More Memories

of

Stockport

The publishers would like to thank the following companies for their support in the production of this book

Main Sponsor
Stockport Grammar School

Chelwood Brick

Deanprint Limited

Elsa Waste Paper Limited

Multi Design Consultants

WM Nelstrop & Company

AG Parfett & Sons Limited

Peak Group

Ramillies Hall School

Rhodia Limited

Frederic Robinson

Sinclair Abson Smith

Sovereign Rubber Limited

Swizzels Matlow Limited

First published in Great Britain by True North Books Ltd
England HX5 9AE

ISBN 1 903204 18 6

Text, design and origination by True North Books Limited
Printed and bound by The Amadeus Press Limited

More Memories

of

Stockport

Contents

Introduction

Stockport, population (1992) 288,900 and covering 49,000 square miles, is one of the Metropolitan Authorities formed in the Greater Manchester 'county' in the 1970s. Like all the other constituent parts of that conurbation, Stockport developed in the late 18th and 19th centuries as an important textile manufacturing town and until 1974 was always thought of as one of the more populous and industrial centres of Cheshire. Indeed it was the very northern boundary of that county and what divided it from Lancashire was the River Mersey. Although that river is always primarily associated with Liverpool and Birkenhead, the Mersey, fed by its tributaries, the Tame and the Goyt, from the Pennines, first becomes a significant flow when it reaches Stockport. Today however it's a matter of chance whether a visitor to Stockport will see the river or not.

How many outsiders come to Stockport to look around? Most people only see it from the windows of a train travelling over the famous Victorian viaduct or when travelling by road along the modern motorway by-pass. A pity because Stockport has much of historical interest to offer the visitor and much in the way of nostalgic reminiscence to offer its native residents.

Finding out about Stockport is very much like opening one of those Russian dolls: a large one on the outside and several others within which get gradually smaller and smaller towards the final little doll in the centre. Present day Stockport is the large outer doll with its multi-storey shopping centre and the inevitable multi-storey as well as ground level car parks that go with it but still preserving, like the Russian doll, traditional features from previous times: in Stockport's case the aforesaid railway viaduct and churches like St Peter's and St Mary's.

Take away this outer shell and the next sized doll reveals Stockport as it was in the 1950s and early 60s. No Merseyway Shopping Centre then but a thoroughfare called Mersey Way built over the river and which, together with Wellington Road South and North, represented the main traffic arteries of the town. There was not one multi-screen cinema but large single ones like the Ritz, Carlton, Super and Plaza with several smaller ones as well in addition to regular live shows at the Theatre Royal on St Petersgate. The third 'Russian' doll reveals Stockport as it was in wartime and the years of austerity in the 1940s: a fantastic cave of an air raid shelter system with trams and tramlines dominating the transport scene. Doll number four gives us a look at the 1930s: an open river flowing through the centre of the town with only two main road bridges across it with Tiviot Dale a main thoroughfare, leading to Lancashire Hill and Lancashire itself, from a town where the majority of people worked in textiles, especially hatting, and lived in terraced houses with few amenities. The last 'doll' is a very tiny one with only a few features remaining as they

The stalls on Stockport's street market in the 1960s

were in past times: when the main road through Stockport was Hillgate - Little Underbank - Great Underbank - Tiviot Dale and the remnants of pre-Industrial Revolution times like Underbank Hall, the Three Shires wine bar and the street market with its medieval royal charter.

Uncovering the various layers of Stockport's past is a fascinating experience. By illustrating these various layers photographically it is hoped that this book will help people to remember and reminisce about their own experiences, or those of older members of their families, and with the help of these reminders rekindle thoughts of times past. More difficult, but perhaps even more rewarding, it is hoped that people who cannot remember these times for themselves or who have not known Stockport until more recent times, will be able to conjure up a picture of what life was like in the town in times past. Whatever the age and circumstances of readers may this book bring enjoyment to whoever reads it.

Memorable moments

I n the many lengthy processes involved in the production of hats, inevitably an employee would specialise in one process from the initial stages of treating the fur or pelt to the finishing processes of blocking, shaping and trimming. In this picture it is the 'forming' and 'hardening' stages which are portrayed. The man in the foreground on the right of the picture is a 'former' and his job was to peel the body of the fur or pelt from the large perforated copper cone on which it had been placed in the Forming Machine and treated by being sprayed with boiling water whilst air was drawn through the cone. The 'hat' was then passed over to the 'hardeners' who in this picture are on the left: their job was to beat it either by hand or by using wooden rolling pins. These two activities were the first stage in the felting process. It was mainly man's work though it is noticed that ladies might also participate. During the forming process the hood of the hat was continually re-aligned and measured to the required shape and size, a different block being needed for each size and indeed for each style. Later the nap was raised, the felt dyed, stiffened and weather-proofed before undergoing the finishing processes of which trimming is illustrated in the pictures on the opposite page.

This page:
Trimming was one of the finishing processes in the hatting industry. A layman reading about how hats were produced is staggered by the lengthy processes it took to produce one

work but then this was 1937 and a time for celebration: the coronation of King George VI and Queen Elizabeth which took place on 12 May in that year. Both pictures show the

hat. Of course more than one hat was manufactured at any one time but the intricate skills and time needed is incredible. In later years many of the processes were mechanised but not all could be and trimming was one of these. Trimming involves having the crown of the hat tied in gauze paper and then ironing it, putting the lining in the hat and fixing the leather binding, and anything else required, into the inside of the hat. All these activities had to be done by hand and this was women's work. Both these pictures show ladies involved in these tasks, looking happy as if they enjoyed their

workshops festooned with flags and buntings and in the one above; a typical piece of northern wit is seen in the topical message that 'Christys Hats cover Crowned Heads'. These pictures and the one opposite were taken in the workshops of Christys Hat Works in Higher Hillgate. Christys was only one of several hat factories in Stockport in the early 20th Century: others included Ward Brothers in the Wellington Mill which is now the Hat Museum, Woodrow and Sons in Adswood Road, William Harrison and Sons in Marriott Street, T. & W. Lees in Adcroft Street and Battersby and Co. in Offerton.

This is a cheerful scene in Robinson Street Edgely in 1953. The flags and the look of enjoyment on the faces of people posing on the pavement outside their homes give all the clues we need to identify the event - the coronation of Her majesty Queen Elizabeth the Second. As can be seen from the wet kerbstones and the fluttering bunting. The weather that day was wet and windy. Over at Woodbank Park more formal events had been planned. The bad weather on the day however ensured that instead of hundreds or even thousands turning up only a few dozen actually braved the inclement weather. In the Town Hall however a different story was unfolding. There more than 1800 people had paid

for a ticket to watch the television coverage of the ceremony. The public may have had to crush into the Town Hall but those who did were not privileged to be joined by the mayor, he was at Westminster Abbey enjoying a far better view of the Archbishop of Canterbury crowning our young monarch. Most folk with any sense stayed indoors out of the rain and wind, many watching the coronation take place on black and white televisions screens with their now long gone 405 lines. Not many of us had a television then, most of us still relied on the wireless for our entertainment and information. Those homes which did possess an early goggle-box found themselves playing at usherettes to bands of grateful relatives and neighbours.

Below: There is nothing quite like Royal Visit. In this case the Royal visitor was everyone's favourite the Queen Mother who came to Stockport on 22nd June 1960. Today the crowds tend to be smaller. One of the theories put forward to explain this is the fact that the television enables us to watch such events without actually attending. But in 1960 the crowds were still on the street! The photographer has captured two views of Great Underbank with photos taken just minutes apart. The Queen Mum had travelled from Edgely Station to the town centre where she visited Christy & Co's premises. What is unusual about this particular photograph is just how few men and children appear to be present; only a dozen or so men being easily seen, the vast majority of the crowd being women dressed in their summer frocks and short sleeves and, confirming the fine weather, the complete absence of that Stockport standby the ever present umbrella 'just in case'. Giving greater emphasis to the fact that the scene is shot in high summer is the clear shadow thrown down the centre of the road. How many of today's readers we wonder recognise themselves amongst this expectant crowd? What became of the small girl standing in the road in her best party frock and now in her forties, older than many of those women around her? And how many of those present that day would have laid bets on the Queen Mother living to celebrate her hundredth birthday?

Right: What on earth could these queues be for. The crowds look as though they are waiting to see someone important. In this case it's the Queen Mum again. The highlight of the Queen Mother's visit to Stockport in June 1960 was her attendance at a reception held in the Town Hall. The crowds were out in force on the Town Hall steps on this fine Summer day. Why is the police constable smiling? We suspect one of the ladies at the barrier has made some remark - perhaps about policemen looking younger every day - this Stockport copper may have been young then but he must have retired long ago by now. The Policewoman sergeant on the right would have been a relatively unusual sight even in the early 1960s; she does not however look as though she would take much cheek from her constable colleague. Wellington Road South disappears into the distance. The view is a little different today - there are far more motor cars to start with. Even in 1960 however there would normally have been quite heavy traffic in the area and given the absence of any other than official vehicles it would appear the road has been temporally closed. The police officer leaning against his car is reminder of happier times when police cars on the road were relatively few and those which did exist kept their roof lights switched on at night so that speeding motorists could see them coming - how times change!

In 1929 old property in Rock Row was demolished and a public stairway connecting Mersey Square and Lawrence Street was built. By 1932 a new art-deco cinema had opened in Mersey Square; the Plaza. The new 'talkies' witnessed a boom in cinema building and conversion of theatres into cinemas. The Plaza was a purpose-built cinema from plans drawn up by W Thornley, architect, the builders, T Collier and Sons of Leigh, used over 500,000 bricks and 60 miles of electric wiring in the course of its construction. The facade was of white terracotta tiling and, according to the souvenir opening brochure, the building was 'a vision entrancing'. A large cinema, even by the standards of its day, it employed a staff of 64 and had a seating capacity of 1,878 in the auditorium which must have been very colourful being decorated in 'gold, silver, deep rose, blues and green.' In the foyer the pay-box was arranged to cope with two separate queues for admission: one for the Stalls and the Lounge, the other for the Royal Circle and the Balcony. Evening prices of admission were seven pence in the Stalls (3p in today's money) and two shillings (10p nowadays), the latter quite expensive for 'going to the pictures' in the 1930s. A Compton Organ was installed (with Mr Chadwick as resident organist) which was to provide musical interludes between the film presentations. The Plaza also boasted a café and restaurant (the decor was apple green) and it was possible to have sun-ray treatment in the Lounge. At the time of writing the Plaza is sheathed in scaffolding and sheeting but in 1960 it was still a very prominent building in Stockport's main square: in 1932 it must have been even more impressive.

Playtime

Above: This is a very clear bright picture, presumably in the early 1950s on a bright Spring or Summer's day. Mersey Square seems far more spacious than it does today with little traffic. Two buses are seen at the bus stops on two of the islands, long since gone from the scene, as is the Furniture Stores on the right side of Rock Row. The cylindrical tower of St Peter's Church can be seen in the upper centre left of the picture suggesting that the photograph had been taken from Wellington Road South, above the 'Bear Pit'. The elegant white facade of the Plaza Cinema adds to the atmosphere of brightness and cleanliness in this picture. The double feature of films showing were 'Innocent Sinners' which starred Flora Robson and David Kossoff, two esteemed British actors of the 1950s and 'Clouded Yellow' which featured Trevor Howard and Jean Simmons.

The Theatre Royal occupied a site on the right side of St Petersgate across from St Peter's Church. It had been built in 1887 to replace the old Temperance Hall which had been destroyed by fire in that year. It was owned by Mr William J Revill who employed the Denville Stock Theatrical Company to perform plays. Their opening show was Shakespeare's 'Hamlet'. It was not all such serious entertainment however. In later years it became a leading venue for Variety and Revues and famous names like Gracie Fields appeared here. In the 1920s several musicals of the time were put on, such as 'No,

No, Nanette', 'Lilac Time' and 'Rose Marie' and these could be seen for the price of 4d in the pit, 7d in the pit stalls, 9d in the upper circle, 1/6 in the stalls and circle and 2/6 for a box. Billy Scott Coomber, a popular entertainer and The Maple Leaf Four, a close harmony singing group were appearing at this time and Staff of the theatre were going off to enjoy a day trip, presumably on a Sunday. The theatre closed in 1957, the last performance being the pantomime, 'The Old Woman Who Lived in a Shoe'. Despite local efforts to reopen it, the Revill Family sold it for £27,000 in 1961: it was soon demolished and a bank built in its place.

Above: The cobblestones, tramlines, the limited amount of traffic and the style of motor-car obviously dates this photograph to about the 1950s. How different it seems today when long streams of traffic from both north and south along this main arterial road and several sets of traffic lights have had to be installed to enable pedestrians to cross. The main point of focus is the Central Library with its dome and flagpole at the corner of St Petersgate. Moving northwards 'down-road' the next building is the Manchester Hotel, more recently named Cobdens, commemorating Stockport's famous MP Richard Cobden (elected in 1841). The most prominent building in the picture is the Carlton Cinema, built in 1937, with a capacity seating of 1,750. It was almost as big as the Plaza but not so large as the Ritz on Duke Street, Stockport's largest cinema which could seat 2,342. The Carlton later became the two screen Essoldo in 1970, the Classic in 1977 and finally the Cannon in 1982. It is possible to date this photograph from the film showing at the Carlton. 'Dishonoured Lady' starred Hedy Lamarr, Dennis O'Keefe and John Loder and was made at the instigation of Hedy Lamarr in1950. The film would therefore be on the circuits either in that year or 1951. Hedy Lamarr was a famous Hollywood star of the 1940s. She had achieved fame or notoriety in a film called 'Ecstasy' made in Europe in 1937: she had appeared nude in a brief scene in that film.

Above right: Simpson Street no longer exists. A small cul-de-sac in the area of Greek Street and Royal George Street, it was a typical late 19th century street of small terraced houses. Originally another row of similar terraced houses like the ones in the picture would have occupied what in 1964 was a stretch of open land. The cobblestones in the roadway and the irregular sizes of the flags that made up the pavements were typical of such streets. The houses were probably built to provide homes (rented of course) for the working class families of such northern towns as Stockport. Such houses would have limited facilities, no garden unless a man-made one was constructed in the backyard, where the main utilities would be a coalshed and an outside lavatory. In 1964 when this picture was taken, the houses seem to have been tenanted by young married couples with families. The open croft provided parking space for one family affluent enough to own a car and would serve as a play area for children. Although the chimney stacks dominate the houses backing on to Simpson Street,one notices that there are no TV aerials as would undoubtedly be the case even on such property at a later date.

Right: A photograph dated 1963, but take away the little boy and it could well have been a depiction of a scene 100 years earlier. The property obviously dates from the 19th Century and by 1963 it was long past its sell-by date. The house in Brunswick Street in the centre of the picture is already disintegrating, having lost many slates from its roof and glass from the windows. Even the houses in Rooth Street on the right of the picture are in a poor state, though still inhabited. Other backyard impedimenta still around in the 1960s include the dustbins, a coal bunker (open fires were still the form of heating in older properties like these and the residue of such open fires would constitute the main contents of the dustbins) and the outside lavatory in the left foreground of the picture. Even the wooden clothes pegs and long clothes props are seldom seen nowadays. The little boy, whose well-turned out appearance strikes the only modern note in the picture is happy to play in this open space, as little boys always are, knowing that Mum can keep a watchful eye on him from the kitchen window.

Below: There is no date on this picture and in poking fun one might be tempted to dub it 'The Von Trapp Family in the Sound of Dickens'. Everything about the picture gives an atmosphere of poverty and pathos: it could have been taken at any time in the early 20th century but one would guess at the 1920s, possibly even early 1930s. It was taken after a rainstorm which adds to the feeling of depression in the picture, the houses possibly had only the one entrance up the steps, but there were cellars beneath, where the coal might be stored. There is little street lighting and the lamp along the pavement in the rear right distance would be a gas lamp, turned on in the evenings by a lamp lighter whose job would take him round several such streets turning on the lamp in the evening and turning them off again in the morning. Despite the miserable surroundings the people in the picture exude an atmosphere of happiness and well being. Their clothes might not be the height of fashion, and it is the style of clothes which seems to place the date in the early part of the 20th century, yet they seem well fed and pleased to be having their picture taken, watched over by the kindly mother or grandma figure in the doorway.

The People's War

Both pictures: This archive photograph *(right)* is dated about 1940 but two pieces of evidence suggest it should be 1939. The parade in the picture looks uncannily like that in the picture above which shows a parade of soldiers marching along Greek Street, giving a salute at the War Memorial. Both are of the 6th Battalion 22nd Cheshire Regiment and in both pictures a brass band is leading the parade. The uniforms and big drum of the band are identical with those in the other picture. Could it be that both these pictures were taken at the same time to record the same event? The second piece of evidence is that the poster on the hoardings on the left side of the picture notifies people that the Princes Cinema is closed for redecoration. William Shenton's book, 'The History of

Stockport Cinemas' states that the Princes was redecorated in 1939. A fair-sized crowd gathered to see this body of troops which had presumably arrived at Edgeley Station and was probably marching to assemble for the parade on Greek Street, shown above. In the late summer of 1939 spirits were high in this country although war had been declared on 3rd September. The war was justified: Hitler had again broken his promise about Czechoslovakia and had refused to withdraw his troops from Poland. Furthermore there was much optimism that 'the war will be over by Christmas' as stated by Sir Seymour Hicks, a well-known actor, in a radio broadcast in 1939. The citizens of Stockport must have felt heartened to see such military strength in their county regiment - a year hence and the outlook would seem very different.

This photograph was sent as a postcard to Anglesey dated 7 August, 1940, by Mr W. Lees. One can only speculate as to the purpose of this procession forming in Greek Street. There are several khaki-clad men and one sailor in the forefront of the parade but also several civilians, mostly of a certain age and wearing campaign medals: one of them towards the rear of this section is carrying a flag which looks like a British Legion banner. The officer with the stick under his arm seems to be wearing a uniform from World War I. It seems likely that these paraders are veterans of that war, some of whom have already joined the Home Guard, (Mr Lees asks on his postcard if his correspondent can 'recognise him,' though his uniform has not yet arrived') but this does not account for the presence of the young sailor. In the rear of the picture a detachment of what appear to be regular troops can be seen but they are not carrying arms. Whatever the occasion it was sufficiently important to attract a fair number of spectators. They give a good representation of how people dressed at the time and from the expressions on their faces this does not appear to be a sad time. By August 1940, people had come to the conclusion that the optimistic forecast of nearly a year earlier that 'the war will be over by Christmas' were wrong and that it was not likely to be true for Christmas, 1940 either. The Battle of Britain had not yet begun and though Britain was now the only country in Europe fighting Nazi Germany, there was a confidence that ultimately victory would be achieved.

Below: The Munich Crisis in 1938 brought home to many people in authority in Britain the distinct possibility of war against Nazi Germany, despite Neville Chamberlain's assertion that he had brought back 'peace for our time'. A prospective road-widening scheme in Stockport had recently revealed many cellars in the sandstone cliffs bordering Chestergate and the Town Corporation decided to create an underground shelter system as protection against any air bombardment. The government refused financial help on the basis that if such a shelter were bombed, the loss of life would be extensive. The Corporation however decided to carry on with the scheme and it was to prove to be a most effective decision. Stockport was to gain protection against aerial bombardment 'without parallel in the region'. The sandstone cliffs were so strong that no shoring up was necessary and so the project proved to be less expensive than had been originally forecast. When complete the shelter was duly inspected by the Mayor and Mayoress and it was first used in the autumn of 1940. It was capable of sheltering nearly 4,000 people but further extensions increased that number considerably. The strength of the shelter became known throughout the region round about Stockport and when the blitz on Manchester began people from outside the borough came into Stockport to use the shelter. The number of these people increased so much that by 1941 residents of Manchester had to obtain a special permit from the Town Clerk of Stockport to allow them to use the shelter. Some people used the shelter permanently irrespective of whether the sirens had sounded or not and it is estimated that in 1941 there were about 200 such 'permanent residents' of the 'Chestergate Hotel'. Wooden benches lined some of the tunnels, there was a sick room and dispensary, staffed by a pharmacist and two nurses with a doctor on call at the hospital, facilities for boiling water and washing-up and even 'flushable' lavatories. Proximity to the nearby main water conduits and drains in Chestergate enabled this luxurious facility of running water. By the end of 1942 fewer people were using the shelter and by the following October it was decided to close it except in case of emergency and they were permanently closed in 1945 at the end of the war. The shelter was reopened in the 1980s to allow special guided tours but today any member of the public can visit the shelter during the regular opening times. It is a very rewarding experience.

Both pages: In 1939 Britain's Prime Minister Neville Chamberlain had made his announcement to the waiting people of Britain that '...this country is at war with Germany.' Stockport, along with the rest of the country rolled up its sleeves and prepared for the inevitable. This war would be different from other wars. This time planes had the ability to fly further and carry a heavier load, and air raids were fully expected. Air raid shelters were obviously going to be needed, and shelters were built in areas such as the sandstone cliffs bordering Chestergate. By the time war was declared an army of volunteers of both sexes had already been recruited to form an Air Raid Protection service. At first ARP personnel were unpaid volunteers but when war broke out in

September 1939 they became paid staff. It was their job to patrol specified areas, making sure that no chinks of light broke the blackout restrictions, checking the safety of local residents, being alert for gas attacks, air raids and unexploded bombs. The exceptional work done by Air Raid Wardens in dealing with incendiaries, giving first aid to the injured, helping to rescue victims from their bombed-out properties, clearing away rubble, and a thousand and one other tasks became legendary; during the second world war nearly as many private citizens were killed as troops - and many of them were the gallant ARP wardens.

At the beginning of the war Sir Anthony Eden, Secretary of State for War, appealed in a radio broadcast for men between 17 and 65 to make up a new force, the Local

Defence Volunteers, to guard vulnerable points from possible Nazi attack. Within a very short time the first men were putting their names down. At first the new force had to improvise: there were no weapons to spare and men had to rely on sticks, shotguns handed in by local people, and on sheer determination. Weapons and uniforms did not become available for several months.

In July the Local Defence Volunteers was renamed the Home Guard, and by the following year were a force to be reckoned with. Television programmes such as 'Dad's Army' have unfortunately associated the Home Guard with comedy, but in fact they performed much important work. The Guard posted sentries to watch for possible aircraft or parachute landings at likely spots such as disused aerodromes, golf courses on the outskirts of towns, local parks and racecourses. They manned anti-aircraft rocket guns, liaised with other units and with regular troops, set up communications and organised balloon barrages.

Other preparations were hastily made around the town. Place names and other identifying marks were obliterated to confuse the enemy about exactly where they were. Notices went up everywhere giving good advice to citizens on a number of issues. 'Keep Mum - she's not so dumb' warned people to take care what kind of information they passed on, as the person they were speaking to could be an enemy.

Older people will remember how difficult it was to find certain items in the shops during the war; combs, soap, cosmetics, hairgrips, elastic, buttons, zips - all were virtually impossible to buy as factories that once produced these items had been turned over to war work. Stockings were in short supply, and resourceful women resorted to colouring their legs with gravy browning or with a mixture of sand and water. Beetroot juice was found to be a good substitute for lipstick. Clothes rationing was introduced in 1941, and everyone had 66 coupons per year. Eleven coupons would buy a dress, and sixteen were needed for a coat. The number of coupons was later reduced to 40 per person. People were required to save material where they could - ladies' hemlines went up considerably, and skirts were not allowed to have lots of pleats. Some found clever ways around the regulations by using materials that were not rationed. Blackout material could be embroidered and made into blouses or skirts, and dyed sugar sacks were turned into curtains.

Both pages: The 1930s were a time when the essential community of people was 'the street'. The majority of people living in towns in the North West lived in terraced housing and the street or (if the street were a particularly long one) a certain section of the street was the neighbourhood to which people felt attuned. With the Silver Jubilee of King George V and Queen Mary in 1935 another Coronation of King George VI and Queen Elizabeth two years later (following the national trauma over the abdication crisis in 1936), the 1930s had two obvious opportunities for such national celebrations.

to have been fine and sunny. Of course not all street parties were held on the same day: School Street, Backwater Street, Portwood and Lloyd Street, Heaton Morris seem to have been favoured with warm sunny weather in which to eat their spam sandwiches and dried egg cakes, whereas the weather seems to have been more chilly in Sandleigh Avenue and the Drive, Brinnington. Despite having to wear top coats and headgear (some of the little girls are wearing 'pixie-hoods' the in-gear of World War II!) One lady managed to concoct a

So it was natural and the expected thing that, despite rationing and austerity, people should celebrate the ending of World War II in this fashion. The German surrender came on 7 May 1945. George VI had been crowned on 12 May 1937 and George V's Silver Jubilee had been celebrated on 6 may 1935. Early May seems to favour such celebrations! From the evidence in these pictures the weather in early May 1945 seems

trifle and another is holding a celebratory cake. May 1945 was a time for great rejoicing in this country: it was the real end of the war. Of course the war in the Far East was to continue until 15 August 1945 when Japan surrendered but Asia was far away and despite European and British Imperial involvement, to many people in this country the war in the Far East had always seemed to be a mainly American affair.

Street scenes

This view of Mersey Square taken from Rock Row above Chestergate, illustrates what the centre of Stockport looked like 40 years ago and it is still easily recognisable today. Other parts of Mersey Square may look very different today from how they appeared in the past but here is one view where today's observer can easily orientate himself. Of course the tall factory chimney dominating the centre background is no longer visible but the railway viaduct is just the same, except that nowadays it would be unusual to see a small goods train moving along it. Sadly such rail transport has been superseded by gargantuan articulated lorries adding chaos to road traffic.

Wellington Road South's sloping bridge is also clearly visible and again the same today, as is the balustrade of the 'Bear Pit'. What is perhaps the most consistent thing about all pictures of this part of the town centre is the end of Chestergate and Rock Row. The railings still look like a parapet and the inevitable taxi-rank on Chestergate always seems to be present: of course the style of the cabs changes as time goes on but if a taxi is needed in Stockport, there always seems to be one (at least!) available at this end of Chestergate. Across the road from the taxis stands the Mersey Hotel (now renamed the Chestergate Tavern) and the road-surface has now been replaced by tarmacadam.

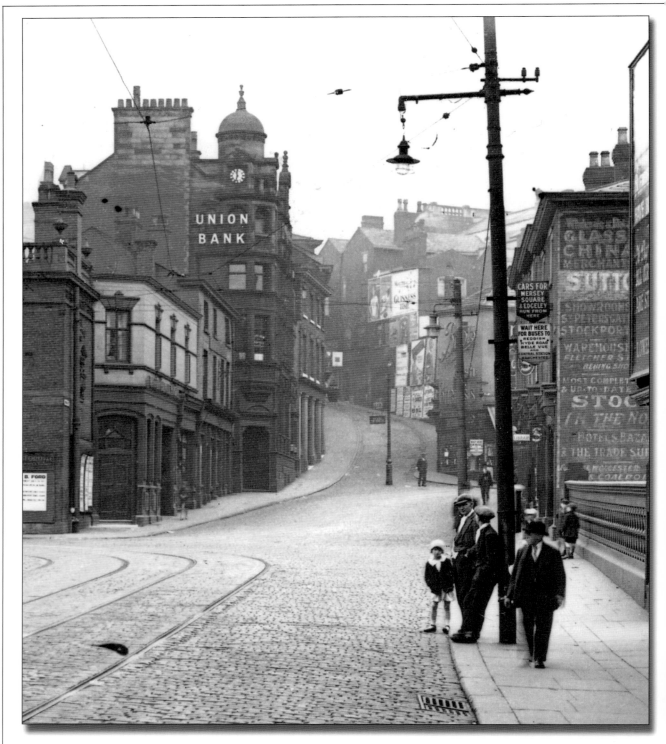

Bridge Street Brow running up in the centre background of this picture and the Union Bank of Manchester with its prominent domed tower are the only means of orientating oneself today in this 1931 scene of Bridge Street. It seems a wide almost deserted thoroughfare (maybe the photograph was taken on a Sunday when the shops like Nathaniel Goulds, first class provisions, and N. Kenyon Morley on the right of the picture) were closed and shuttered. Today on Bridge Street one does not think one is walking on a bridge over the River Mersey but in 1931 that was obvious: children can be seen looking through the parapets of the Lancashire Bridge (hence the name of the street) down to the river, perhaps hoping to see a salmon leap: salmon are reported as being caught in the river in the early part of the twentieth century. Most of these buildings have been demolished, including the Warren Bulkeley Arms; its distinctive facade on the centre left of the picture has been partly incorporated on to the building behind it which recently housed the Laura Ashley shop, and the former lord of the manor's arms are clearly visible on the top of that building. The fine stone edifice of the Union Bank remains but now houses a menswear shop. Warren Street going off to the left of the picture now has Barclays Bank on the corner, built on the site of the old Buck and Dog public house.

Above: Stockport's famous Town Hall in the background still seems dominant in this photograph of the main south-north arterial road through the town. Two parked cars and one motor cycle are the only vehicles visible: there are no double yellow lines forbidding road-side parking and no traffic lights - just one pedestrian crossing. The Garrick Hall is still with us but the retail shops shown have all disappeared, as has the Super Cinema, now replaced by the Royal Mail's main sorting office. The Super Cinema dates back to 1910 when it was opened as the Stockport Electric Cinema. In 1921 it became the Super and was one of the leading places of entertainment when talkies were developed in the 1930s. Unlike the purpose-built cinemas of that decade however, the Super had no café or refreshment kiosk so a page-boy was employed to go to a nearby shop to buy cigarettes and sweets for the cinema's patrons. 'Going to the pictures' was a prime activity of people in the 1940s and undoubtedly the privations of wartime added to its popularity. In 1941 it was suggested that cinemas should be allowed to open on Sundays in Stockport but the local authority refused permission. However in 1944 cinemas were allowed to open on Red Cross Sunday in May to raise money to help prisoners of war. There were 29 cinemas in Stockport in the 1940s: by 1962 there were only 14. The Super closed in 1965. Today Stockport has only one cinema, the multi-screen complex in the Grand Leisure Centre, quite near to where the Super once stood.

Below: A wide expanse of open road with only one or two motor vehicles visible date this photograph either in the early part of the day, on a Sunday or at least in the mid 20th century. Regardless of the day or time of day, it is the idea that it is from some time ago that is most convincing. There are tram-lines in the road and tram-wires above and there is a sign on the lamp-standard/telegraph pole on the right of the picture which says that trams will stop there by request. It does seem that the man on the pavement is waiting for a tram and as the very last tram ran in Stockport in 1951, it is almost certain that this is a picture from the 1940s or 1950. The white building behind the man on the right of the picture is the old Toll House and before the building of Wellington Road in the early 19th century there was a Toll Bar near Chapel House (the building on the opposite corner of the road from the Toll House is called the Chapel House Hotel).This toll bar would be at the northern (Lancashire) end of what was then the main south-north road through Stockport. This ran via Hillgate, the Underbanks, Lancashire Hill and Manchester Road, the toll bar at the other (Cheshire) end was on Hillgate at the corner of Mottram Road, opposite 'Toll Bar' Street. Toll bars were established by turnpike trusts in the 18th century to charge tolls from travellers using the roads they had built: the money was levied to offset the costs of construction and to maintain the roads in good condition.

A view of the eastern side of Wellington Road South - this scene was maybe taken later in the day than the previous one: there are certainly more people about. Vehicular traffic seems very sparse - a box-like small saloon car and two or three commercial vehicles but if this was 1940, few families would possess a car, even a small one, and this was wartime. Petrol rationing would soon impose severe restrictions on private car use, indeed many such cars would be unusable as the rubber tyres were needed to help the war effort and larger saloon cars were taken over by the government to be converted into ambulances and transport vehicles in the armed forces. The relatively new Carlton Cinema and the much older Manchester Hotel (now Cobdens) stand out clearly below the junction with St Petersgate and on the opposite corner of that road is the Central Library. The Library was built in 1913 after Andrew Carnegie, an American millionaire of Scottish descent, offered a gift of £10,000 to Stockport for the purpose of building a free library. Starting in Dunfermline, his native town, in 1880, Carnegie gave large amounts of money for free library provision in both the USA and Britain. Stockport employed an architectural firm from Bolton who estimated the cost at £14,000. Carnegie offered a further £5,000 providing Stockport agreed to spend £2,000 to build a branch library in another part of the town. The Central Library was built by E Marshall & Sons and opened on 14 October 1913.

Right: Some parts of Stockport have changed very little over the last few decades and here is one such view, taken from in front of what was then the Mersey Hotel, since renamed the Chestergate Tavern. All pictures of this end of Mersey Square show the taxi rank at the end of Chestergate, the railings above, the large building on the opposite side of Rock Row and the billboards. Nowadays the posters do not advertise Capstan cigarettes as displayed here but recommendations to drink Guinness and to eat Heinz Beans are still with us. Stockport Village Craft Centre and a physical fitness studio now occupy the large building on the right of the picture and there are still retail shops in the lower part of the premises. Walking up Rock Row towards St Peter's Square is still the same but the property at the top of the hill is no longer there and has been replaced by much more modern buildings.

Below: In this 1960 view of the eastern end of Mersey Square a double decker bus is seen at one of the 'bus-stop islands', no longer there of course, and the ever-present taxi rank is there at the corner of Chestergate on the Rock Row side of the street.

Similarly the Mersey Hotel (now the Chestergate Tavern) is on the opposite corner of Chestergate. The property on the right hand side of Chestergate is still extant and within this block stands the present-day Tourist Information Office. Mersey Square looks very different and far more compact today than it does in this picture: there seems to be so much more 'elbow-room' in 1960! Even Rock Row leading up to St Peter's Square seems more spacious. The large factory-like building which was Ormespers Furniture Stores still looms large and there are still shops on that side of Rock Row but the main function of this building nowadays is as the premises of Stockport Village Craft Centre and as a fitness gym. The hoardings further along Rock Row are still there but the domestic buildings at the back are no longer visible.

Below and right: These two views of Mersey Square are virtually identical. The picture below is precisely dated as April 1960 but there is no date on the one on the right. Also the one below shows more of the western side of the square, the other more of the eastern. Mersey Square had been reorganised in the 1930s and Mersey Way, constructed as the main entry to it from the east, was opened in 1940. The end of Mersey Way can be seen in both these pictures on the far right side, emerging into the square between the Mersey Hotel (now the Chestergate Tavern) and the old Tramway Offices. Beyond the Tramway Offices, especially in the picture on the right, the old Fire Station is clearly seen and beyond that the end of Princes Street with its low level range of shops at its western end. The larger buildings on the right of course would all disappear in the 1960s when the new Merseyway Shopping Centre was built. On the skyline in both pictures, the spire and church of St Thomas, Heaton Chapel, stand out - the church is no longer there but the spire still dominates the horizon when looking northwards from this part of Stockport. To the left of the church, the chimney of E Axon Ltd., Builders Merchants, also stands out but this is no longer there - nor is the instruction to 'buy UCP tripe' on the white-fronted building below it. Both pictures show the 'Bear Pit' and also bus-traffic still using the square: buses may still be seen driving through the western part of the square, but much less frequently nowadays, as the number of bus-stops in these pictures indicates. Finally the tower of the supplementary tramway depot, built in 1924 and later also used as a bus depot, and situated at the junction of Heaton Lane and Wellington Road, can be seen on the left side of picture on the right.

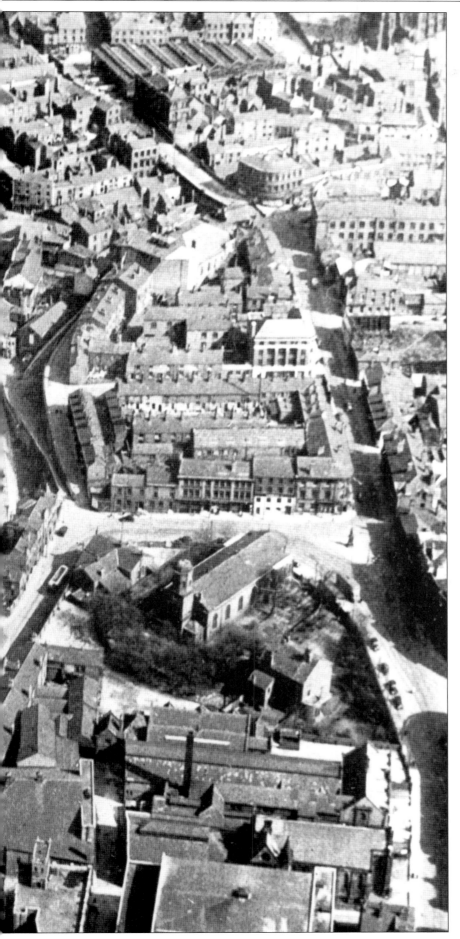

An aerial view of Stockport town centre today would in some ways look very different from this view taken around 1950, yet it is still possible to orientate oneself as several features remain the same. Perhaps most obvious in this respect is St Peter's Church and churchyard on the right hand side of the picture, and behind it, standing isolated, is Cobden's statue in St Peter's Square. From here St Petersgate runs to the top of the picture with the bridge over Little Underbank standing out clearly. Beyond and to the right of this, in the very top corner of the picture, can be seen the lower half of St Mary's Church. In the centre of the picture running parallel to St Petersgate, Chestergate can also be clearly seen: at the lower end of it on the left is the Mersey Hotel, since renamed the Chestergate Tavern, and the long edifice of the Co-operative Society's department store, now the Sunwin Chestergate Centre. Chestergate runs through towards the upper middle of the picture and merges into the narrower Great Underbank. To the right of Chestergate, running up to St Petersgate, Rock Row also stands out clearly. The wide arterial Mersey Way with its pronounced curve on its lower end has since been overlaid with the Merseyway Shopping Centre: gone are the sheds of the Tramway Depot along its flank and the old Fire Station which in this picture front Mersey Square. Consequently the long straight line of Prince's Street, then the main shopping thoroughfare of the town, stands out very prominently on the left of the scene. Many of the old buildings have been demolished or redeveloped but the Plaza Cinema is one that remains: its roof and the top of its facade seen in the bottom right centre of the picture.

Bottom: Cars can no longer be seen on the part of Bridge Street shown in the foreground of this picture: it is now pedestrianised. This picture must have been taken in the 1960s, certainly before the completion of the Merseyway Shopping Precinct we know today. Although vehicles can still be seen in the part of Bridge Street leading to Tiviot Dale and turning into Warren Street on the right of the picture, traffic is much more limited now than it was then, but even then priority had to be given to vehicles crossing Bridge Street from either Warren Street or Merseyway as the Halt sign on the left of the picture indicates. Partly because of the reduction in the amount of traffic using this area today, it seems much more light and spacious but the new brick building also give the place a much more light and modern appearance.

Right: A No. 16 bus from Manchester has arrived at what was probably its terminus in Mersey Square in 1963. Ironically that terminus was right in front of the building which had origi- nated as the Tramway Office. Behind this building were the large tram-sheds which can be seen in the aerial photo- graph on the previous pages. Petrol-driven buses had appeared in the 1920s in Stockport and in 1934 the

first double decker was introduced but it would have been of a much older vintage than the bus in this picture. When this bus-route was first developed buses did not travel the whole way. A ticket could be bought in Stepping Hill to take one as far as Stockport and then another one had to be purchased to continue the journey into Manchester. Even in 1963 the bus driver was virtually concealed from the passengers on his bus: tickets would be bought from the conductor who presided at the rear of the bus, not from the driver whose job was to drive the bus. Will we in this country make the next move and have to buy tickets from a shop before boarding.

On the move

The old pre-war bus station in Mersey Square behind the Wellington Hotel shows a rather disconsolate group of people. Although double-decker buses had been introduced by the North Western Bus Company in 1934, it appears from this picture that single deckers were the norm. Buses of course were not the only form of public transport as evidenced by the tram-lines in the bottom right hand corner of the picture. There is no doubting the date of the picture also from the clothing of the potential passengers. Most people are wearing hats and the ubiquitous raincoats if not worn, always tended to be carried by the men. The young boy, perhaps 11 or 12 years old, was wearing short trousers as was usual in those days for boys of that age. The Wellington Hotel which looms so prominently in the background no longer exists under that name though the building can still be noticed behind what is now McColls kiosk selling stationery and confectionery.

Above: The lack of clarity and definition in this photograph in addition to other evidence seems to date it to the early part of the 20th century. The dress of the men and particularly of the boy standing in the road in the lower right of the picture almost make it look like a picture from the late 19th century. That cannot be, however, as the first electric tram was only introduced into Stockport in 1901 and it ran from Mersey Square to Woodley Station. Horse-drawn trams had operated in Stockport since the 1880s but electrification made trams the 'gondolas of the people'. A smooth and easy ride, electric trams enabled people to travel to and from work more quickly and cheaply and to make visits out of town: it was said that the countryside began where the tramlines finished. Of course the system was limited because trams ran on flanged wheels on a pre-laid iron track and the electric power was supplied by a cable-rod connecting with the overhead wires. Originally the upper deck of a tram-car was open to the elements and was sometimes approached by an outside staircase; seats were usually wooden but later upholstered seating and roofs over the top deck were introduced. Despite the advantages, tramways with their static middle-of-the-road tracks and overhead wiring system impeded other vehicles on the roads. A limited attempt to introduce trolley-buses failed to withstand the impact of petrol-driven buses in the 1920s: these buses were the death knell of the 'people's gondolas' Surprisingly tram-cars remained until after World War II (the last tram-ride was in 1951) and with the developments like the Metrolink and the escalating price of petrol, Stockport may once again see these magnificent vehicles on its streets.

Right: Perhaps today people think of the Merseyway Shopping Precinct as the central hub of Stockport but before that was constructed and opened in 1970, Mersey Square was the obvious focal point of the town. And very busy it was, especially with road vehicles, in the 1960s when this picture was taken. The construction of Mersey Way, opened in 1940 and leading directly into the square and traffic from Wellington Road, both South and North, meant that a lot of vehicles converged on Mersey Square. Although traffic still comes into the square today, it now seems a comparatively quiet area. In the 1960s, buses, lorries, vans and typical family saloon cars of the time, like the Ford Anglia, Morris Minor and what looks like a Triumph Herald in this picture, were regular visitors to Mersey Square. The Plaza and the large building to its right which then housed a furniture store and is today home to 'Stockport Village' dominate the far side of the square and the tower of St Peter's Church can still be seen from this vantage point but one can no longer board a bus from the pavement of Wellington Road as was possible in this picture.

Below: Dominating this picture of Mersey Square in the period immediately following the second world war is the presence of public transport. Only one privately owned car, and that may well have been a taxi-cab, is seen but there are seven or eight buses and climbing the incline of Wellington Road South is a tram-car. Buses already dominate the scene (the last tram-car ride would take place less than four years after this picture was taken and the overhead tram-wires would also disappear). Public transport would provide much employment in 1947 as each bus and tram-car would not only require a driver but also a conductor. In the background, the tall factory chimneys give evidence of what was Stockport's main source of employment at this time: textiles, and the arches of the famous railway viaduct, then as now, appear very prominently.

Right: Not many people today would recognise this picture as one of Mersey Square. It was taken in the 1930s. It could be any corner and street junction in any small town. Yet here stands a police officer on point-duty (he is wearing the white over-sleeves to enable road-users to see clearly the directions he would give to keep traffic moving), so a certain volume of traffic was expected in this location. Many other features in this picture point to it having been taken before the second world war. The box-type saloon car emerging into Mersey Square from the left reminds one of the getaways made by James Cagney and Humphrey Bogart in the gangster films made in the 1930s. It looks as though the car might be for sale but the sale notices are not stuck into the car roof but are on the shop-window behind it. This sale was of fur goods. Furs and real animal furs were the height of fashion in pre-war days. The 'fox fur' was one such fashion accessory: a lady might appear to be carrying a dead fox over her shoulder, its glass button eyes peering at one above its mouth which would be clasping a cord from the body part, its tail hanging down the back of the lady wearing it. Tramlines on the cobbled roadway and tram-wires above also date the picture as does the clothing worn by the people on the pavement: all are wearing hats and the older lady beyond and to the right of the policeman is wearing clothes of a length that must have seemed old-fashioned even in the 1930s.

Bottom: It is very difficult to recognise Chestergate as it is today from this picture taken on Boxing Day 1966. A well known Guinness poster appears on the side of the shop on the right of the picture and Greenall Whitley advertise their wares on the side of a double decker bus. Petrol driven buses had been introduced into Stockport in the 1920s (though there had been trolley buses before that time) but these were single deckers: double deckers only arrived on the scene in 1934. These buses were the North Western buses which would later be incorporated into the Greater Manchester organisation. Though occupying the background in the picture, Stockport's famous railway viaduct dominates, as it does most views of the town. This notable piece of Victorian architecture and civil engineering dates from 1840 when a viaduct 1,786 feet long and 54 feet 4 inches wide were constructed to take a double line railway track above the town. The viaduct comprises 22 main arches of 63 feet span and four of 22 feet span, 111 feet above the River Mersey. The first passenger train crossed the viaduct in 1842 in the decade when 'Railway Mania' seized Britain. In 1887 the viaduct was widened to take four lines of traffic and is still used by services between Manchester and London as well as many others.

Right: Wellington Road, both South and North, was built in the early 19th century as a by-pass road to relieve the pressure on what had always been the main south-north route through Stockport, i.e. Hillgate, the Underbanks and Lancashire Hill. By the 1960s the traffic on this by-pass was very heavy as is still the case today. Perhaps this picture was taken at 'rush hour' with people going to and from work as there are pictures of Wellington Road South when the road seems calm and empty. Furthermore, the majority of motor vehicles at this time were small private saloon cars or vans: only one or two larger lorries can be seen and certainly none of the heavy articulated vehicles one sees today. The spire of St Thomas' Church on the skyline is still a prominent feature today but the factory chimney alongside is no longer visible. Neither is the clock tower in the very centre of the picture - this was part of a new supplementary tramway depot built in 1924 at the corner of Heaton Lane and Wellington Road on the site of the former gas works. This depot was also extended in 1932 to house over 100 buses which by that time competing with trams for public transport services.

Mersey Way, the great new arterial road into the centre of Stockport had been completed and opened to traffic in 1940. Its aim was to relieve the pressure of traffic entering the town via Princes Street, the main shopping thoroughfare, and Great Underbank and Chestergate. It was a further development of the first main culverting of the River Mersey between Wellington Bridge and Mersey Bridge which had been completed in 1935. To culvert the whole of the remaining stretch of the river flowing through the town centre was a spectacular undertaking in those days. This huge building project used portal frames of re-inforced concrete built into the solid sandstone of the cliffs of the river banks, overlaid with secondary beams and then 'decking' to carry the finished road. Occasionally work on the project was hampered by flooding of the river, notably in January, 1937 but eventually the work was completed and officially opened in 1940. Ironically with the petrol restrictions of wartime and immediately afterwards in the years of austerity, the impact of the new road was not felt until the 1950s and 1960s, when the volume of traffic using the road showed a marked increase. No doubt these women shoppers, warmly wrapped up against the weather would not appreciate the benefits of Mersey Way at this particular time and saw the increased volume of road traffic as a nuisance. Mersey Way has seen much bigger changes since this picture was taken but Susan Smart, the Ladies Shop on the corner is still there!

Building on the past, preparing for the future

A long and distinguished academic tradition began in Stockport even before Christopher Columbus discovered America. Lessons at what later became Stockport Grammar School commenced in St Mary's Church in the market place in 1487. For more than half a millennium it has operated as a local school, educating children from Stockport and surrounding districts, and on several occasions it has intersected significantly with the history of the nation.

The founder, Edmond Shaa, had something of a distinguished history, having travelled from Stockport to London to make his fortune and becoming, in Dick Whittington fashion, the 200th Lord Mayor of London as well as court jeweller to three kings of England. He was Mayor when Richard Duke of Gloucester usurped the crown of his young nephew Edward V. In June 1483 Shaa's brother, a cleric at St Paul's Cathedral, preached a keynote sermon proclaiming Edward a bastard. Three days later Shaa himself led a deputation from the City of London to Richard and implored him to take the crown. Two weeks afterwards, he was crowned as Richard III and his first act as King was to knight Shaa. Whatever the nature of the plot which put him on the throne, Shaa was in it up to his neck.

Top: *John Bradshaw, ex-pupil of the school and president of the court that condemned Charles I to death.*
Right: *Sir Edmond Shaa, Lord Mayor of London and the school's founder, offering the crown to the future Richard III.*

When Richard III proceeded to reveal himself as a serial killer of his own relatives, however, Shaa realised he had backed the wrong horse. Being a skilful political operator he swiftly realigned his loyalties, managed to survive the defeat of Richard at Bosworth and became a firm favourite of the victorious Henry VII, first of the Tudors. By 1487 his good fortune enabled him to found a school in the town of his birth. He endowed it with land and made the Goldsmiths' Company, of which he was a member, its trustees. For a salary of £10 per annum a priest was to pray on Wednesdays and Fridays for the souls of Shaa, his parents and all Christian people. The priest doubled as schoolmaster and the other part of his duties was to educate a cross-section of local children. He directed that the 'said connying Preest kepe a gram schole continually in the said Towne of Stopford

Above: *The building at the junction of Greek Street and Wellington Road, which housed Stockport Grammar School from 1832 to 1916.*

and teche allman persons children that woll com to hym to lerne, after their capaciteys that God woll geve them'. His motive was partly selfish, since the main duty of the scholars was to reinforce the priest's twice-weekly prayer sessions and swell the ranks of those pestering God on Shaa's behalf. But the upshot of this was that one of the oldest schools in the country was founded.

Shaa could not have known that within sixty years of his death the avalanche of the Protestant Reformation was to sweep down on his Catholic school. Because it had been founded as a chantry (so called because its chief function was to chant prayers for the dead founder), the Reformers roundly condemned it as superstitious. The school was saved only when the Goldsmiths' Company paid the government the Tudor equivalent of £3m to allow it to continue. But by a complicated legal process the Company secured ownership of land in the City of London which Shaa had left to fund his local school. Without the Reformation, it would have been the richest school in England.

A century later an ex-pupil of the school made a devastating impact on the turbulent events of the mid-17th century. This was John Bradshaw, who was born at Wybersley Hall on High Lane and attended Stockport Grammar School before being called to the Bar at Gray's Inn. He leapt to stardom when he became President of the court which tried Charles I in 1649. Sitting in a bullet-proof hat, he condemned the king to death and was the first to sign his death warrant. Once England was a republic he became President of the Council of State, the highest office in the government. As such he was President of the only republic in English history. After the restoration of the monarchy, however, his rotting body was exhumed, his head was displayed on a pike and his reputation suffered accordingly. The word 'traitor' was scrawled next to his name in St Mary's parish register and the man who should have become a left-wing hero was effec-tively deleted from the historical record.

In 1745 Bonnie Prince Charlie, the Young Pretender, landed in Scotland to rally support for the exiled Stuart dynasty against the ruling Hanoverians. He collected an army of Highlanders and marched on England. The rebels were well on their way to London when they descended Lancashire Hill and crossed the vital bridge over the Mersey north of Stockport market place. The pupils of the Grammar School, then situated in Chestergate, were allowed to skip lessons and watch the intruders pass through the town. Like the rest of Stockport's population, they did so without open hostility but also without much enthusiasm. What the Highlanders wanted was volunteers for their army and perhaps the lukewarm response of spectators from the Grammar School contributed to a crucial sample of opinion. Shortly afterwards, they lost heart and turned back to Scotland. Their cause already defeated, they were destroyed on the battlefield of Culloden.

In the 19th century, Stockport ceased to be an insignificant northern market town and became part of the new cotton metropolis of Manchester. This should have done what Bradshaw failed to do and put the school on the map. Instead local mill-owners were unimpressed by its obsession with the civilisation of Ancient Greece and Rome - a classical education was fine for southern boarding schools but not for gritty northern 'grammars'. The school celebrated its 400th anniversary in 1887 with a grand total of 17 pupils.

Below: *The first Speech Day in the quadrangle of the new building during the first world war, with many of the older boys already in uniform.*

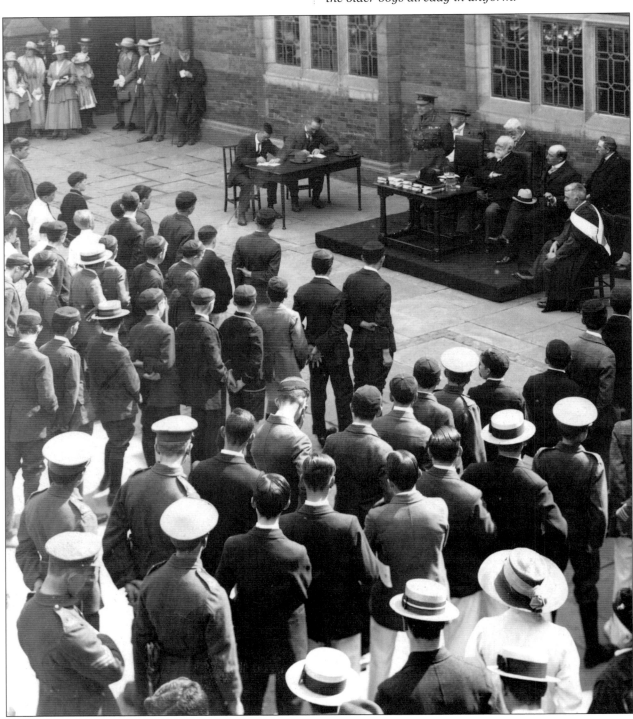

In the 20th century the school was saved from impending doom by adapting itself to the educational needs of a growing and prosperous local community. In 1916 it started on the road to expansion by quitting its cramped site in the town centre and acquiring the present buildings at Mile End.

A major step towards academic acclaim came in 1902 with the appointment of Alfred Daniels as Headmaster. Daniels, a first-class Cambridge mathematician, introduced changes which led to greater success in public examinations and university entry by SGS pupils. For the first time, numbers of Old Stopfordians at Oxford and Cambridge climbed into double figures. The race for places at Stockport's by now most prestigious school was on and by the mid-1930s 380 pupils were crammed into a building designed for 250. Public school status was granted in 1933 and accompanied by

innovations designed to promote *esprit de corps* - a house system, team games, sports day, speech day, school societies, school trips, school uniform, a school magazine, a school orchestra, a school choir - and even a short-lived school song.

World War II brought radical changes. Masters were called up and replaced by women, refugees arrived from Manchester Grammar School, nights were spent fire-watching instead of sleeping, gas-masks were carried at all times and pupils swiftly learned to make rude noises with them. Cellars were used as air-aid shelters and for a time homework and Saturday morning lessons were cancelled. The school buildings themselves escaped major bomb damage but school games became impossible to play owing to unexpected arrivals on the playing field. These included obstacles to thwart landings by German paratroops and sheep acquired as a substitute for fuel-guzzling motor-mowers. In 1946 the names of 60 ex-pupils who had lost their lives were inscribed on the War Memorial, joining those who had perished in World War I.

Top: *The present school at Mile End, opened in 1916.*
Above centre: *The arms of the Goldsmiths' Company, set in a wall of the 1916 building.*

The 1944 Education Act gave SGS 'direct grant' status, which entailed putting a quarter of its places at the disposal of neighbouring local authorities in return for a grant from the government. A new Junior School was launched in a converted Victorian house in Davenport Park, and Headmaster Frederick Philpot gave the school a period of consolidation and stability during the 1950s. A Headmaster's House was completed in 1954 at a cost of £4,621 5s 10d. It was named, unsurprisingly, Shaa House.

Headmaster, Francis Scott enjoyed change almost as much as his predecessor hated it. The school reverted to independent status on the ending of the Direct Grant system in 1976, a change which necessitated the doubling of school fees. Funds were raised to secure subsidies for pupils of limited means and this prompted closer links with the community as well as with parents through the Parents' Association, contacts which had been formerly discouraged. For the first time in two generations building recommenced with new classrooms, new gym and new assembly hall on stilts over the drive. Under Junior Headmaster Richard Reeman the old Junior School was demolished and rebuilt to the latest educational design, as it became clear that SGS must safeguard and expand its own source of entrants to the Senior School. The school's continuing association with the Worshipful Company of Goldsmiths was given public recognition in 1972 when the New Hall was opened on Founder's Day of that year by Viscount Amory, the Prime Warden of the Company.

Changes on the Board of Governors now gave those with a bold vision the advantage over those too cautious to take risks. In 1979 an opportunity was seized and the adjoining Convent School, about to close, was purchased. Girls were admitted in 1980 and the Senior School reached its present complement of 1000 pupils, with a Junior Department of 260 (now 450). Other similar schools followed the co-educational trail successfully blazed by SGS and delegations arrived from rival establishments to see how it was done. This era of expansion was crowned by a visit from HRH the Princess Royal to celebrate the Quincentenary of 1987.

Since then, building has never stopped and an ongoing programme has changed the Buxton Road frontage beyond recognition. As recently as twenty years ago the school lurked almost unseen at the end of a narrow drive. Now perimeter walls have been lowered and vistas opened out. A new clock tower and dining hall can be glimpsed, while wide gateways

Above centre: *Boy meets girl in the newly co-educational school of 1980.*

last century invented the computer, ran a national newspaper and conquered Everest. The school's role as pioneer in independent co-education and its steady ascent in the league tables of academic excellence have given it a national reputation.

Yet unlike the handful of medieval foundations which rival its antiquity, notably Eton and Winchester, SGS has remained the local grammar school that they all once were. It is proud of its association with the town of Stockport and genera-tions of local children from every kind of background. In the 18th century it educated the sons of local gentry alongside the offspring of yeomen, tradesmen and labourers. It has no intention of celebrating the 21st century by becoming a school for the rich. It will continue to offer the finest education to all who can benefit, true to the founder's command that his schoolmaster was to 'teche allman persons children that woll com to hym to lerne'.

welcome rather than repel visitors. The Junior School has been twice enlarged, the latest upgrade showcasing a magnificent new facade, and a state-of-the-art Sports Hall is in the pipeline. Bigger and better facilities have been matched with broader educational opportunities. Science has expanded and the curriculum has incorporated new subjects like Psychology and Business Studies. The computer revolution has been eagerly embraced and Information Technology integrated into most subjects.

Sometimes setbacks overshadowed successes. In 1997 New Labour's abolition of the Assisted Places Scheme (intro-duced in 1981) once more threatened to restrict entry to pupils who could pay. The solution has again proved to be Bursaries to subsidise those who cannot, but the scale of funding required poses a real challenge for the future.

So Stockport Grammar School enters the third millennium with resources, pupil numbers, academic opportunities and success beyond the dreams of the planners of 1916. Of its five centuries, the twentieth proved its greatest. Old Stopfordians of the

Above left: The new quadrangle of 1991, designed to mirror the old. Above right: The new Hall of 1972, which re-launched the building programme with modernism on stilts. Below: The new Junior School of 1998.

At the shops

Not a busy scene of Stockport Market in 1961, but 1949 was the period of austerity following the second world war when rationing of various goods was still in force. Nevertheless the market stalls seem to have ample produce for sale. This picture also gives a glimpse of the covered market hall built in 1861 of glass and cast iron and nicknamed 'the Glass Umbrella'. The basis of this structure is much the same today but a century after its being built the local authorities decided to modernise the market area. The 1960s appeared to 'swing' in many ways and regenerating outmoded areas in towns was certainly part of the swinging scene, Stockport most noticeably. In this modernisation process sometimes buildings of historical interest can be demolished and regretted afterwards. Fortunately Stockport Heritage Trust has managed to oppose the demolition of the notable Staircase House in the market area. Will other buildings like the Covered Market be thought to be in need of alteration in the future and will the street market traders find it economically viable to continue their business in the light of growing competition from supermarkets and buying and selling on the Internet? There is an ambience about market trading however that these more modern methods will never replace and the demand for a street market, first made in 1260 will probably still be there in 2060.

On turning into Hillgate from Edward Street, there is a private car park and the first building one comes to comprises a narrow doorway with signs on the wall indicating that on the first floor one will find the office of the Training and Manpower Services and on the second floor, Olliers Solicitors. Some years ago one would have found Briggs' Cycle Shop on this site. Here might be purchased anything that a cyclist might need and at prices which today seem ridiculously cheap: Dunlop Fort tyres at 10/6 (53p), an inner tube at 3/- (15p), etc. The enterprising advertising by the management urges customers to fit new tyres for Easter, a time when keen cyclists would be eager to ride out of Stockport into the country lanes of Cheshire or for the more adventurous into the Pennines of Derbyshire and South Yorkshire. Briggs sold whatever such stalwart adventurers might need: rucksacks, cycle capes, spare handlebars as well as the tyres and inner tubes. If a new bicycle was needed, customers were encouraged to ride the 'New Hudson for Business and Pleasure'.

Above: Looking along Great Underbank from the building that once housed the Union Bank of Manchester but is now a Menswear shop, this view of the ancient 'main road' through Stockport, has changed little in appearance from what it was thirty years ago: except that the occupiers of the shop premises have changed. On the right side of the picture, Lloyds Bank (now Lloyds TSB) still occupies the building that projects out on to the pavement but the other shops have been taken over by the National Westminster Bank which also occupies Underbank Hall. The next building however is yet another part of Lloyds Bank. Apart from a café bar, a photographic shop and a charity shop, the only break in the bank monopoly is an amusement arcade! It may be very convenient for banks to monopolise this section of Great Underbank as Building Societies do the other part but whether this fulfils the criteria of the Civic Trust to integrate 20th century requirements into an earlier architectural environment creating an area which is attractive and pleasurable to be in is a matter open to question.

Above right: Taken on a spring day in 1961 this view of Tiviot Dale is still easily recognisable today thanks to the buildings structure having remained much the same. The rear of the picture however indicates that in 1961 Tiviot Dale was a road leading up the rise to somewhere else. Today there is no doubt that Tiviot Dale is a cul-de-sac. The King's Head public house remains a prominent building but Sheargolds electrical goods shop has been replaced by the HFC Bank. Bowfields is no longer in the block between the bank and the King's Head: instead there is a 'filling station' which does not provide petrol but filling for hungry and thirsty people, and a wool shop. Beyond the King's Head the dwelling houses have been replaced and a large office complex now dominates that end of Tiviot Dale. On the other corner of Tiviot Dale the Tobacconist's urging people to smoke 'Bestem' is now the Stockport Bullion Company. The pair of male pedestrians in the picture display the typical 1960s garb of raincoat and hat.

Below centre: At the time of writing Mealhouse Brow is almost completely inaccessible. Pedestrians can walk from Little Underbank up Mealhouse Brow to the Market Place but the whole of the top section of the alleyway is completely concealed by scaffolding: the old properties are being demolished to make way for a block of flats and a few ' retail outlets'. No. 11 is at the bottom of the brow and is no longer the spic-and-span electrical goods shop shown in the picture but a run-down property for sale. Indeed the only business premises open on Mealhouse Brow today is the newsagents next door at No. 9. An evocative name, Mealhouse Brow is derived from the time when the meal house was at one end of the passage and a baker's at the other. In 1961 when this picture was taken, White and Swales Ltd. must have seemed in the height of fashion with TV sets as well as radios. No videos or CD players are on sale but one could buy all makes of records and tape-recorders - how modern!

Bottom: Taken just over a year after the picture on the previous page and from an angle that shows more of the other side of the street and its continuation towards Lancashire Hill, this photograph of Tiviot Dale in 1962 shows much more activity on the road. A bus is coming down Tiviot Dale towards Bridge Street which would be impossible today and other motor vehicles are obviously using Tiviot Dale as a through road. Before the construction of the fast track of Knightsbridge and Great Egerton Street as we know it today, Tiviot Dale continued towards Lancashire Hill and together with Bridge Street must have been one of the main entries into Stockport. The retail shops and King's Head are still clearly visible on the left of the picture and the Tiviot Hotel across the road is still there today. Public houses in Stockport as elsewhere seem to have a longer lease of life than retail businesses and of course always sell the same commodities.

This view of the stalls on Stockport's street market of around 1960 is little different from what one sees today as far as the stalls and surrounding buildings are concerned. The main difference might be mainly in the clothes of the shoppers: the ladies shopping in 1961 are dressed most elegantly. The right to hold a market in Stockport goes back to 1260 when the Lord of the Manor was granted a Royal Charter by King Henry III. The manorial lord was given the right to charge tolls on anyone selling goods in the market and he appointed officials to collect them and to ensure that the market was properly conducted. On the sixth hundredth anniversary of the granting of the Charter, Stockport Corporation bought the manorial rights from Lord Vernon, whose family name is commemorated in several features of Stockport. In 1851 the Corporation built the new Market Hall, often referred to as the Farm Produce Hall or Hen Market (one can readily visualise the activities that went on inside it) and the front of this imposing building occupies the right side of this picture. Originally a single storey building the upper part with its neo-classical columns and balcony was added in 1875. In the mid-nineteenth century, this civic building acted as a town hall and the announcement of election results took place from the balcony. The varied architecture of the neighbouring buildings provides an interesting contrast in styles from the mock Gothic of the building next door, then the Italianate white facade to the mock Tudor building apparently housing an opticians in 1961. Dewhurst's butchers shop at the end makes no pretence to be anything other than it was.

Both pictures: Taken from Lower Hillgate on a sunny September day in 1961, the image on the left shows little difference from the one above which had probably been taken some years before. The picture on the left has a fuller and better span, showing property on both sides of Little Underbank but the main difference seems to be in the depiction of the building immediately behind the St Petersgate Bridge. The scene above shows quite a prominent top storey on the building but in the 1961 picture this seems to have been removed and replaced by an advertisement hoarding. At the time of writing Little Underbank is being refurbished but otherwise the buildings, regardless of changing trading enterprises in the shops, are virtually the same today and represent one of the most nostalgically interesting parts of Stockport.

The St Petersgate Bridge is one of the most impressive features of Stockport civil engineering from past times. When proposals for the bridge were first mooted in the 1860s they were opposed by shopkeepers on the Underbanks who feared it would cause them to lose trade. Eventually however the bridge was opened on 24 February 1868. It is still a great vantage point enabling one to look down on to the architecture of the 18th and 19th centuries below and its newly decorated parapet is a pleasant and colourful part of the urban landscape. The most famous premises seen from the bridge of course are those which originally were Jacob Winter's Jewellers. The name Winters still stands out prominently from above the windows of what is now an eating and drinking place. It was in 1880 that Jacob Winter decided to move his business from Hillgate to these premises in Little Underbank. For a jeweller perhaps, security was the main consideration. The building had no rear entrance (it still hasn't) as it was constructed directly into the rock, so any entry and exit had to be made through the front of the premises. Furthermore Mr Winter installed a unique security device for one of his display windows (presumably where his most expensive items were exhibited). This took the form of a mechanism hydraulically operated by the natural spring water available in the rock and it enabled the window and all its contents to be lowered into the shop cellar. Nowadays the 'shop' windows display pint glasses of beer being raised by customers to the establishment but on the outside of the upper storeys of the building it is still fascinating to observe the famous clock and the Victorian figures of a soldier and a sailor strike their bells on the hour and half-hour. They stand on each side of the figure of Father Time with his white beard and traditional scythe, though in this representation he looks particularly well-fed and for some reason is sporting angel's wings on his back. A pedestrian standing in Stockport's Little Underbank might easily imagine himself in a medieval town in Germany where such mechanical time-pieces are prevalent.

In 1961 Stockport Council and Chamber of Trade met architects from the Civic Trust and Design Partnership to hear their suggestions for fulfilling the aims of that body which were to make the best of the high overall standard of architecture: 'to integrate 20th century requirements into an early 19th Century setting and to make the area as attractive and pleasurable to be in' as possible. This picture was published in the Stockport Advertiser in September,1962 with an article containing the previous quotation. One might ask today if they succeeded in fulfilling the aims of the Civic Trust. The cobblestones have been tarmacadamed over and the buildings made more modernised in appearance but Great Underbank

in this picture has become mainly a street of Building Societies and Banks. Stoddards shop on the left of this picture is now the Yorkshire Building Society and the buildings on the other side of this part of Great Underbank now house the Nationwide, Woolwich, Alliance and Leicester and Cheshire Building Societies. Only at the very end of this row do we find a break in this 'mortgage monopoly' when we reach the Country Larder. To be fair, the building immediately preceding the Yorkshire Building Society is the Three Shires wine bar, a redoubtable bastion of pre-Industrial Revolution style of architecture, echoed further along in the structure of Underbank Hall. May these examples of individual historical interest remain.

Making a living

This photograph shows the Avro aircraft production line at Woodford. The world's most reliable turboprop engine, the Rolls Royce Dart, powered the Avro 748. The 400 orders for the 748, which sold in over 50 countries, kept the Woodford factory occupied throughout the 1960s and 70s. It was in 1908 that Alliot Verdon Roe became the first Englishman to fly when he flew his bi-plane for 150 yards. In 1910 a company established to manufacture aeroplanes took his name AV Roe. The Avro airfield at Woodford opened in 1925. At the outset there was no water or electricity on the site, the latter deficiency only being remedied in 1933! The massive New Assembly facility would eventually cover over a million square feet and became an ideal aircraft production facility. The name Avro is indelibly linked with planes for the RAF. The Avro Anson for example first went into service in 1935 with the last example delivered to the RAF in 1952. Over 11,000 Ansons were built. By 1942 the Woodford factory was however turning out the famous Lancaster bombers at a rate of seven per day. The first Shackletons came off the production line at Woodford in 1950. The Shackleton continued in service until the 1970s when it was replaced by the Nimrod as the front line reconnaissance aircraft used by the RAF. In 1952 the most amazing sight was the first delta-wing Vulcan Jet bomber taking off from Woodford; the Vulcan became the backbone of the Strike Command for over two decades.

Below: In the 19th Century when the river Mersey flowed through the centre of Stockport, the only bridged crossings from the south side of the river (Cheshire) to the north side (Lancashire) were the Lancashire Bridge from Bridge Street into Tiviot Dale and up Lancashire Hill and the Wellington Bridge carrying the main by-pass road from the south to Manchester. In the 1900s Mersey Bridge was constructed to link the two parts of Mersey Square which were on either side of the river. In the 1930s it was decided to culvert the whole stretch of the river between Wellington Bridge and Lancashire Bridge. This was done in two periods: the first culverted the section between Wellington Bridge and Mersey Bridge and it is in this development that this picture was taken. In the top left quarter of the picture can be seen the arches of the tram-car depot which was built in 1902. The parapet is the downstream one on Mersey Bridge. The workmen can be seen erecting the reinforced concrete support arches which would carry the nearly extended road-surface of Mersey Square. This development was completed by 1935 (a plaque on the upstream side of Wellington Bridge denotes the fact) and in 1936 it was decided to continue the culverting from Mersey Bridge to Lancashire Bridge, inaugurating the new thoroughfare of Mersey Way which was completed in 1940.

Bottom: Taken from the CWS building in Chestergate this photograph, taken on a winter's day in 1966, clearly shows the momentous work involved in the construction of the new shopping precinct. Within thirty years of that gigantic undertaking the citizens of Stockport were to witness a further spectacular change in their town. Merseyway which had been built to ease the flow of road traffic into Stockport was to be dispensed with and replaced by a huge shopping complex to meet the needs and demands of the 1960s when economic recovery after the second world war and the years of austerity was beginning to attract such developments in many towns in Britain. Marks & Spencer, Woolworths and British Home Stores which can be clearly seen across the centre of the picture were now to do an 'about turn' as previously their main entrances had been on Prince's Street, but today it is the entrances on Merseyway that are most frequently used by customers. As a result of this development the construction of the Knightsbridge - Great Egerton Street by-pass and the M63 (M60) enabled through east-west traffic to avoid passing through Stockport but extra car-parking was needed in the town to cope with the requirements of shoppers.

Above and right:
The first 'modern' reorganisation and regeneration of Stockport town centre occurred in the 1930s. The picture on the right shows the giant cranes at work in the culverting of the river in preparation for the building of what was to be nicknamed 'the Bear Pit'. It was a spectacular feat of civil engineering but one that was organised so as not to disrupt the daily traffic and business

of the town centre. The trams and tram-lines could not be disturbed, nor could the overhead cables without which the trams could not run. Inevitably such a large undertaking attracted a number of spectators. In the picture above the building on the lower left was functioning then as an information office for the buses: it is now a newsagents and snack shop. Perhaps this photograph was taken earlier in the day and certainly at a different period of the construction from the other: only one large crane is now in situ and the wooden buttresses have been attached to the Wellington Road

Bridge. The buses in this picture however undoubtedly date this as the 1930s: they are single deckers and with a very box-like design - 'streamlining' was to come later. In the background of both pictures can be seen a row of shops at the western end of Prince's Street, which was then the main shopping thoroughfare of Stockport. Prince's Street is named in honour of a visit to Stockport by the Prince of Wales, the future George V in 1908. It still remains part of the main shopping complex, though somewhat overshadowed by the Merseyway development.

What are these women doing? And what do those mysterious numbers hanging from the ceiling indicate? Lots of readers will know, many of them having worked for Philips Semiconductors in Hazel Grove. And why are there no men in view - surely a case for institutionalised sex discrimination if the identical scene were to be captured by the camera today? Given the absence of surgical masks we can guess that some kind of solid state devices preceding the micro chip are being worked on at the benches. The premises may look huge and intimidating and the workers set out like battery hens but that is definitely a misconception. Facing one another the girls could talk and chat. And despite the 'Brave New World' look some things seem to have been carried over from earlier factory traditions: if one of the girls was getting married her colleagues would sing all day - something they would also do at Christmas when lunch was served in the canteen by the factory managers Philips Semiconductors had its origins in what was once a furniture factory in School Street in Hazel Grove. The firm was originally known as Salford Electrical Instruments later becoming part of GEC and acquiring extra premises in Broadstone Mill at Reddish. The business became part of Mullards in 1969 a year before the move to the site at Pepper Road in Hazel Grove. The name Philips Components was adopted in 1988 reflecting the move away from valves to silicon chips.

Over a century and a half of brewing excellence

For six generations the Robinson family has maintained an important brewing tradition in Stockport, starting out from the town centre Unicorn Inn in 1827. Frederic became landlord of the pub in 1859, taking over from his parents, and though initially trading solely as a retailer, he soon entered the beer brewing business, which was entering a growth phase. He was successful from the start and at the time of his father's death in 1875, he was the owner of a substantial brewery. He also took the first steps in ensuring that Robinson ales were sold in the best possible condition by purchasing a small number of public houses, which became exclusive outlets for Robinson ales.

From 1876 Frederic started to expand the Unicorn brewery and introduced up-to-date brewing equipment to cope with increasing demand. At this time he also became the local distributor for Arthur Guinness Son & Co, Dublin.

Above: Frederic Robinson (1836 - 1890).
Right: The Church Inn, Cheadle Hulme, one of the earlier pubs acquired by Robinson's in the 1880s.
Below: Women workers during the Great War.

His son William had grown up learning the brewing business and was able to take over the day-to day running of the business, helped by his brother Herbert, when Frederic died aged only 54 years in 1890. William's chief contribution was to encourage the production of fine ales. From the brewery at this time came Old Tom Ale which was the achievement of Alfred E Munton, Head Brewer, and who married into the Robinson family. Alfred kept meticulous notes of the brewing processes. He purchased the Company's first microscope so he could examine yeast and beers and he conducted experiments to test the keeping qualities of the ales.

The brewing industry went through difficult days at the start of the 1900s when there was a general decline in ale consumption, partly attributable to the Temperance Movement. However, Robinson's which had not joined the trend in massive retail outlet acquisition suffered far less than many others, and William was in a good position to expand the Unicorn Brewery. The company now had a product range of six beers.

The company went into a period of expansion. New Brewery offices were built around 1913 and two years later the assets of a local competitor, John Heginbotham's Borough Brewery were absorbed into the Robinson empire. By 1918, all three of the fourth generation Robinson sons had joined the family business. William's eldest son, Frederic, gained a B.Sc with honours in Chemistry and was later to complete a master's degree making yeast the subject of his thesis - this expertise was subsequently used for the benefit of the company when Frederic opened the company's first laboratory and introduced production control into the brewing process.

The decision, taken in 1920, to become a private limited company was a recognition of the fact that the business needed a more formal financial structure but one that retained full family control over the whole brewing operation. William became Chairman and Managing Director and his son, John, who had recently qualified as a solicitor entered the family firm.

The early 1920s saw an extensive programme of pub purchases as a strategy to address the twin problems of plummeting beer consumption and the availability of the alternative attractions of the cinema and radio to the beer-drinking public; in this climate only those pubs which could shed their image as urban drinking holes could hope to prosper. In 1926 William appointed his three sons, Frederic, John and Cecil to the Board of Directors, and later that year acquired Scholfield's Portland Street Brewery of Ashton-under-Lyne. In so doing the company acquired forty-two new pubs in an area previously not covered by Robinson's as well as a wine and spirit business, which was later developed by Cecil.

By 1930 the brewery plant had been completely upgraded and a new brewhouse built under the supervision of Frederic who

Above: A selection of labels, drip mats and advertising material used by the firm over the years.
Top: An outing from The Bridge Inn, Chestergate c 1914. The Bridge Inn was Frederic's first customer.

specified the most advanced equipment available at the time. Built adjacent to the original brewery, its seven storey tower bearing four large red unicorns is still a landmark in Stockport today. Robinson's had also bought Kay's Atlas Brewery of Manchester. John Robinson initiated a programme involving the alteration and refurbishment of the company's public houses. This and the wide choice of drinks available to the customer thanks to Cecil's efforts on the supply of spirits to the business contributed to the continuing success throughout the difficult 1920s and 1930s.

It was John also who took on the responsibilities of Chairman following the death of William in 1933 and under his leadership the company continued its steady progress through the difficult years of the 1930s depression. This was chiefly due to John's policy of investing in the acquisition of pubs in the countryside surrounding Stockport and Manchester, which had been the traditional area of distribution for Robinsons

Above: Distinctive bottles used by Robinson's in the 1920s. Right: The original Church House a few years before Robinson's acquisition in 1929. Below: A horse-drawn dray as used by Frederic in the 1870s.

ales; these included pubs as far afield as the Derbyshire Dales and the first house in North Wales in 1943. This was a particularly astute business move since it was in contrast to the inclinations of their competitors. The move made it possible to attract a different clientele and proved to be vital to the future success of the company.

The brewing industry operated under special difficulties during the World War II when brewing materials were restricted and there were increases in beer duty as well as labour shortages, but fortunately the brewery and all but one of the Robinson pubs (The Railway in Wilburn Street, Salford) escaped damage from direct bombing hits. By contrast Boddingtons Breweries Ltd of Manchester suffered a serious loss when their Strangeways Brewery was destroyed in December 1940. Robinsons was among the twenty-two local breweries which helped them out until the rebuilding of the brewery was complete in August 1941 - Boddingtons took their casks to the Unicorn Brewery to be filled with Robinsons beer and then delivered it to their customers.

However, the Unicorn Brewery did not come out of the war totally unscathed; in November 1943 there was a serious fire which took the National Fire Service three hours to bring under control. Fortunately the new brewhouse

was untouched and the vital stocks of malt escaped significant damage. The brewery was able to restart production within a week.

Government restrictions began to ease after the war and once again Robinson's was in a mood for expansion. In 1949 Bell & Co Ltd was taken over. Bell's assets included a brewery, 155 pubs and off-licences. This purchase was the largest undertaken by Robinson's and made the company the largest brewer in north Cheshire.

In spite of the war, the adventurous pub acquisition policy continued and in 1943 the first of what was to become a substantial estate in Wales was purchased.

The 1950s saw Dennis and Peter, two of John's sons join the company - they were the fifth generation of Robinsons to carry on the family tradition. In 1958 John received a knighthood for political and public service in Cheshire. John's third son, David joined his brothers on the Board of Directors in 1966.

The number of brewing companies dwindled rapidly in the 1960s as small businesses were taken over by larger concerns; of the 6,447 breweries known in 1900, there were merely 358 at the start of the 1960s; by 1968 this number was 220. Improvements to the business were essential to keep the company abreast of the rest of the

industry and during the 1960s - a kegging plant was added and a new bottling plant was constructed in Ashton Road, Bredbury.

Sir John, who had devoted over 50 years to the Company, died suddenly at his desk in February 1978 and was succeeded as Chairman by his son, Peter. Pub refurbishment and when opportunities arose, the purchase of additional houses and the building of new houses has continued, including the acquisition in July 1982 of Hartleys (Ulverston) Ltd, a long-established Cumbrian brewery with its 56 houses and its leading brew, XB.

Over recent years further phases have been developed at Bredbury with all packaging and deliveries now emanating from there. Five members of the sixth generation are now actively involved with the business and Best BITTER and OLD TOM continue to win awards.

Above: Sir John Robinson burying a time capsule in the foundations of the building for the bottling plant in July 1974. **Right:** *Part of today's fleet.*

A sweet success story

Swizzels Matlow Limited is the largest employer in the New Mills area, having a workforce of over six hundred. It is the UK's leading independent supplier of children's sugar confectionery. The company is still essentially a family concern. The sons of the founders, Alfred and Maurice Matlow and David Dee, are still actively involved as Directors of the company and have now been joined by members of the third generation of the family.

It was in 1928, in a small London factory, that Matlow Bros Ltd started production of table jellies, and jelly type confectionery, Jolly Lollies, Cello Fruit, Milky Bars and Butternuts. Alfred and Maurice joined forces with David Dee in 1933 to form Swizzels Ltd, starting out in a factory at Star Lane, Canning Town, London E16 and in the same year moving to larger premises in

Drivers Avenue, Plaistow, London E13. Swizzels Ltd specialised in the manufacture of fizzy sweets in compressed form, Dimple Mints, Navy Mints and Cashoos, which over the course of time developed into the present-day nationally known range of Love Hearts, Sherbits, Fruit Fizzers, Double Lollies, Parma Violets, New Refreshers Chews and Drumstick Lollies.

In 1940 both companies, having suffered damage in the Blitz, evacuated to a dis-used textile mill in New Mills, Derbyshire. The mill was about one hundred and fifty years old at the time but had been extensively rebuilt after a fire in 1883. These premises are still in use today, now transformed to accommodate offices and stores. Throughout the intervening period steady development of business, both at home and abroad, has necessitated considerable expansion of both production and warehouse facilities. A new factory was opened in 1971 by the Lieutenant of Derbyshire and new production plants for fully automated manufacture were installed. Recognition of Swizzels' success

Above left: *An advertisement dating from 1965.*
Below: *Part of the fleet in the 1950s.*

This is the same commodity most of us have in our kitchen cupboards but it is delivered to the factory by the tanker load, 19 tons (19,307 kilos) at a time. This is then blown into the factory holding tanks. The sugar is next put through the sugar mill, which turns the granulated sugar to icing sugar, this is the basic ingredient for tablet production. The icing sugar is fed to mixing machines where colour, flavours and other products like citric acid and bicarbonate of soda (which helps to give the fizz) are added. After this has been thoroughly mixed, it is ready for the tablet machines. Some of these machines will compress up to 5,000 tablets a minute. After the tablets have been compressed they are mixed to get an assortment of different colours and are then conveyed to the various wrapping machines, which enclose the sweets in their familiar livery.

Drumstick Lollies and New Refreshers Chews are made from the same chewy base which is made by mixing together sugar and glucose (technically corn syrup), adding a little fat and gelatine and boiling it up to 126 deg C. The batch of chew is then placed onto the table and allowed to cool, the batch is put through special wrapping machines, which can wrap at speeds of up to 800 sweets a minute and are packed into boxes to be taken away to the warehouse from where they are distributed to the wholesalers and subsequently to shops.

came during that year when it was awarded the Queen's Award to Industry for Export Achievement.

Sweet production on Swizzels Matlow's scale is a vast undertaking and is based primarily on sugar.

Above: *An exhibition stand thought to have been Olympia in the 1930s.* ***Top:*** *A lorry taking part in a local procession in the late 1940s.*

Another type of production is called Panning. This is a method of coating sweets with sugar. A pan comes in various sizes anything from 3 ft to 6 ft in diameter, it can best be described as a saucepan

revolving on its side. The method of production is to revolve the sweets in the pan and gently pour a sugar syrup over the sweets. When the required thickness of coating is obtained the pan is emptied and the next load is put in.

Towards the end of 1974, further production warehousing was needed and a factory extension of 40,000 sq ft was completed. In 1976 production and warehouse space was obtained when the old Paper Mill, known as Grove Mill was bought. It was in this year also that the company adopted the title of Swizzels Matlow Ltd, to symbolise the complete integration of the two companies.

In 1984, the company was honoured to receive from the British Safety Council, the 'Sword of Honour' making them one of an elite group of only thirty companies throughout the world to receive this award for having a lower accident record than any other company in their industry. Acclaim and recognition also came in the form of the 'Fit for Work' Award in 1986, for outstanding achievements in the employment of disabled people.

Indeed providing good working conditions has been a feature of the company since it inception. This is demonstrated by the fact that it still a number of employees with a lifetime of service to the company on its payroll. Consideration for Swizzels' pensioners was extended on a very special and proud day for the company when on 14 June 1990 it was host to a visit from HRH Diana, Princess of Wales. Three ladies, who between them had clocked up over 125 years service and had worked in the original London factory and stayed in New Mills after being evacuated there during World War II, were given a grand-stand view of the Princess as she arrived at the factory.

It was a red-letter day attended by employees past and present and three hundred schoolchildren all excitedly clamouring to catch a glimpse of the Princess. A posy of flowers was presented to Her Royal Highness by Joan Parker, who with a record of forty-six years

Above: *Princess Diana's visit to the company on June 14th 1990.*
Top: *An early staff gathering.*

service as sweet packer and supervisor was Swizzels' longest-serving employee. When the Princess heard how long Mrs Parker had worked for the company she said, 'I should be giving flowers to you!'

Directors Trevor Matlow and Michael Dee gave the Princess, who confessed to having 'a sweet tooth', a tour of the factory. She was allowed in the top-secret 'Fizzyology' Dept and watched Fizzers and Double Dips being produced. She stopped at the Love Heart machine and witnessed the production of some very special sweets. A limited edition of Love Hearts bearing the inscriptions 'Princess of Wales', 'Prince of Wales', 'Prince Harry' and 'Prince William' was being manufactured. These sweets were not for sale and after a supply had been given to Diana, who thought they would prove popular at home, the rest of the 'one-off' packets were given to 2000 local school children, as a souvenir of the day. Though these particular names will never be used again, the Love Hearts brand remains one of the most popular in the

company's history. Manufacture of the sweets is now automated and the machines mould and stamp two million love hearts per hour. The secret recipe remains exactly as it always has done, but some of the messages have changed over the years - 'Cherry Lips' and 'Wacko', have long been discontinued as have 'Fat Cat' and 'Wow', popular in the 1960s. But 'Kiss Me', 'Marry Me', 'Be My Love' and 'I'm Yours' remain as favourites among the brand's cheeky mottos.

In 1995, a Distribution Warehouse was purchased at Adlington, Near Poynton, to ease the pressure on accommodation at New Mills.

Swizzels Matlow's products are found in thousands of sweet shops throughout the country and are hugely popular, but this is certainly not a matter of chance. A massive programme of advertising in leading children's comics such as The Beano and The Dandy, which reaches jointly a readership of over one million children each week is undertaken. Television advertising on prime-time Children's TV takes place throughout the year in joint advertising with the magazines and through this medium over 20 million children are reached. The company is constantly looking out for ways to stay ahead in the race to be number one children's sugar confectionery specialists. New products are under consideration all the time and great efforts are expended on keeping the brand names atrractive and in up-to-the-minute packaging. The company is committed to offering quality products at value-for-money prices.

Above left and right: *Swizzles Matlow's range of confectionery.* ***Left:*** *The New Mills premises.*

A business with bounce

Rubber has a thousand uses from erasing pencil marks to forming complex parts for industrial machines. One of Stockport's most important firms is Sovereign Rubber, a business which has specialised in this remarkable material since the 1950s.

The firm was founded in 1955 as Rubber Reclamation Northern Ltd by Alan Snell, the father of Vincent Snell who would subsequently run the firm for more than 20 years.

Alan Snell and his fledgling firm began as rubber brokers, taking in salvaged rubber from shipwrecks amongst other sources. At the outset the business was run with just four people working from a small garage in Dukinfield

before later moving to Gee Cross, Hyde where the firm stayed for four years under the name of Snell Reed Trading.

Sources of rubber were varied but a regular supplier was the Receiver of Wrecks, part of Customs and Excise, from whom the firm bought salvaged rubber from wrecked vessels from as far away as Devon, the Isle of Man, Orkney, Caithness and Stranraer. Other regular sources of scrap rubber in that period were the Dexine Rubber company in Rochdale, Ferodo in Chapel-en-le Frith and Swintex of Bury.

Some of the firm's earliest customers were Batley & Co in Stockport to whom they sold rubber tubing, Carborundum at Trafford Park which bought rubber compounds, Futura Rubber at Stalybridge which made golf balls; rubber sheets were sold to Lindsay & William's in Openshaw whilst BTR at Leyland bought moulded ebonite battery cases.

Above centre: *An exhibition stand from 1999.*
Below: *A 1990 Reddish Carnival float from Sovereign Rubber.*

Just as in its early days, the company is still processing rubber, manufacturing compounds and extruding rubber into various sections; only the scale had changed: 3,000 dies are kept on site to produce different extruded rubber shapes. A specialist moulding press for rubber matting is also used. Of increasing importance also being manufactured at the Sovereign works are synthetic coloured granules made by mixing, curing and granulating rubber which is then used in making sports, athletic, safety play surfaces and commercial flooring.

The main properties of rubber are its long life, durability, weather resistance and energy absorbency. To those qualities Sovereign Rubber adds vibrant colours and boasts approval by all major authorities such as the Centre For Sports Technology in London, Germany's FMPA and IST, Labosport in France and Austria's OIST.

Today the firm's main products are marine fenders, equine mats, specialist extrusions, and materials for playgrounds, theme parks, running tracks and flooring.

Trading as BRG International the firm is a world wide supplier of coloured EDPM rubber granules for sports, recreational and industrial and commercial surfaces. When manufacturing the EPDM rubber the colour, hardness and specific gravity are checked to ensure consistency and adherence to specification as each batch is produced. When the finished rubber is granulated testing begins again and both colour consistency and adherence to size specification are verified; on site laboratory facilities test such properties as tensile strength, breaking strain and resistance to wear; similarly to ensure that the firm's rubber granules can withstand the effect of differing climatic conditions

In was only in 1982 that the company completed its move to its present location in Stockport: the Sovereign Works at the Hillgate Industrial Estate. The premises had previously been occupied by Murray & Ramsden Tank Lining although originally, or at least around the time of Queen Victoria's death, the site was home to a hat works.

Before the move to Stockport the firm had been looking for new premises for some time. The premises which are now the Sovereign Works were ideal since they already had had two 60 inch rubber mills in place so they could start production immediately. At first the firm occupied only one of the industrial units there but when other units became available the firm took them until by 1982 they had the whole site. Today the firm employs just under 100 staff.

Above and top: *The firm's premises today.*

they are subjected to extremes of sun and rain simulated at the Sovereign Works in an accelerated weather tester.

BRG International rubber granules are found in sports stadia all over Britain including the UK National Stadium at Crystal Palace, the Meadowbank Stadium in Edinburgh, White Hart Lane football ground. Overseas BRG's granules have been used as far away as Chile, Puerto Rico, Sweden and New Zealand as well as in several sites in the USA including the University of Arkansas, the Naval Academy in Maryland and the Olympic Trial track and field facility in New Orleans where six world records have been set on BRG granules.

Interestingly the company has an important customer in the USA which is part-owned by the Dodge family of Lancaster, Pa, who by coincidence originate from the Stockport area and are well known to local historians.

Sovereign's sales are mainly to installers of safety surfaces, commercial flooring manufacturers, sports surface installers, marine installation contractors, horse box and trailer manufacturers and owners.

For horse owners Sovereign's rubber stock mats are hard wearing, slip resistant, hygienic and cost effective alternative to using straw in trailers and stables - and so confident is the firm of the quality of its product that it offers a ten year guarantee!

Over the years Sovereign Rubber has successfully diversified from being a small commercial extrusion manufacturer to become one of the UK's largest and most innovative manufacturers of general rubber products catering for a wide range of industrial applications. A typical product for example is wheel chocks for the aviation and transport industries; the triangular chocks are rounded at the corners to prevent damage and are heavily ribbed on all three sides to prevent slippage; similar processes can produce a variety other products such as D-Buffers - rubber bumpers used on light goods vehicles, wagons, loading bays and pillars whilst double D-sections made from a hard wearing compound specifically designed to absorb energy on impact are made as protective wall strips to prevent damage to structures and property from HGVs, stacker trucks and vans.

In these days when no office is complete without a cat's cradle of cables snaking from computers, printers and other equipment, running dangerously across floors and ever-ready to trip the unwary, Sovereign Rubber manufactures cable and hose protectors to allow cables to be safely ducted across floors or roadways. The same extrusion process used to manufacture such products is also used for making a whole range of rubber door seals for containers.

Above centre: *Fenders in place at Bristol.*
Top left: *Rubber fenders leaving the factory.*
Top right: *A large cylindrical fender installation.*

Having began business taking rubber from the sea it is perhaps fitting that the firm should now make many products for the oil and gas industry, docks and shipping concerns: rubber pipeline blocks are used by the North Sea oil and gas industries and rubber fenders are used in docks and on tug boats throughout the British Isles as well as on ships throughout the world.

The business faces fierce international competition from such firms as Melos in Germany, Kraiburg in Switzerland, Avon Rubber in Britain and also from manufacturers in the US and the Far East. Even so the company aims to be the leading world supplier of specialist rubber products for niche applications by offering a top quality product and a service which exceeds customer expectations.

But rubber is not always the only thing in the company's corporate mind: for two years in the late 1980s it was the main sponsor for Stockport County FC. Another 'outside interest' came in 1989 when the firm had a float in the Stockport Carnival built by the staff at Sovereign Rubber and came second in its class. The following year they entered Reddish, Marple, Glossop, Stockport and Hazel Grove carnivals winning at Stockport and Hazel Grove. The float was built by John Cleary and Donald Bailey: John is one of the firm's longest serving employees having completed 21 years, only Malcolm France with 22 years under his belt beats him.

Sovereign's entrepreneurial spirit has its rewards; in 1991 the firm received the Queen's Award for Exports. By 1997 the firm which began life in a garage was number 74 in the Sunday Times list of the UK's 100 fastest growing privately owned companies: David Wood Sovereign's current MD was presented with the award by Richard Branson at his home in Oxfordshire. Nor was that the end: in June 2000 on the Insider List of the top 50 fastest growing private companies in the North West Sovereign Rubber came in at number 30.

In an evermore cynical world it's wonderfully reassuring to discover that at least the rubber Sovereign makes turns out to be worth its weight in gold!

Above left: *An example of the firm's playground surfacing.*
Below: *Sovereign's sponsorship of Stockport County FC.*

The stuff of life

Who first had the idea of grinding the seeds of wild grasses to make flour is unrecorded. Milling was a skill already old by Biblical times, with its origins thought to be in Mesopotamia. One of the earliest methods of milling grain was a simple pestle and mortar succeeded by a hand powered circular mill. It was however heavy work and demand for animal, water and wind powered machinery to take away the drudgery soon led to the development and building of such technology.

In more recent times, in England, the monopoly ownership of a flour mill was an important privilege often granted to the Lord of a Manor who could require all his tenants to pay for the privilege of using his, and only his, mill to grind their corn.

By the 19th century however such restrictions had become part of ancient history; there was a free market in milling if not yet on the purchase of corn in world markets. Millers whose ancestors had once worked for their Lord worked for themselves, and some were doing very well for themselves.

Lancashire Hill in Stockport has a long history of flour milling. When a new suite of offices was under construction at Nelstrops Albion Mills, a heavy millstone was unearthed there, a reminder of the windmill which once stood atop the hill.

It was on that same spot that 19 year old William Nelstrop set up his corn dealing business in 1820. He came from a long line of Yorkshire farmers, millers and corn factors stretching back at least three hundred years.

When William married the daughter of a local miller he linked two successful businesses and set the pattern for the Nelstrop family firm today, six generations on.

The firm's foundation year of 1820 pre-dated Stephenson's first passenger railway line from Liverpool to Manchester - and Daimler's first petrol

Above left: *William Nelstrop, founder of Wm Nelstrop & Company in 1820.*
Below: *A line drawing of Albion Mills , taken from an original invoice heading.*

driven motor car by 57 years. One, or sometimes two, real horsepower reigned supreme and when towards the end of his working life William Nelstrop returned to his native Yorkshire he commuted to Stockport on horseback until his death in 1877.

William Nelstrop had moved into the steam-powered Albion Mills a year after they were built. He became an important local figure serving as Mayor of Stockport and was offered a knighthood by Queen Victoria for his part in defusing the anti-corn law riots of the 1840s. William turned down the knighthood partly because of his sympathy with the poor who were starving because they could not afford to buy bread and partly because lower wheat prices would benefit his own business.

The original Albion Mills were destroyed by fire in 1893 and rebuilding provided the opportunity to replace all but one of the stone grinding mills with state of the art 'Henry Simon' steel roller mills.

During the second world war all the central Manchester flour mills were destroyed in air raids. The remaining mills in the suburbs stepped up production to meet demand for flour. Nelstrops

William turned down a knighthood because of his sympathies with the starving poor

introduced three shift work schedules whilst family members and staff stood by with sand buckets on the roof to douse incendiary bombs.

The mill escaped damage but then faced the difficult years of the 1950s ad 60s as mergers and amalgamations led to many small firms disappearing, taken over by national conglomerates. Before the war there had been 250 milling companies today that number is less than 25 - a case of the survival of the fittest.

Today, using wheat from the UK, Canada, the USA and Europe, Nelstrops produces 50 different types of flour and 120 different products such as special Pizza Lily Flour sold nationally through wholesalers to meet the increasing demand for pizzas. Demand for other specialist 'ethnic' food products of all kinds is increasing too whilst main customers are independent bakers, brand names and pre-packed own labels. At least seven different kinds of white bread flour are offered, three wholemeal flours, two brown flours, three malted flours, four soft flours as well as flours for such things as cakes and batter.

Above: *The flour mill in Ackworth, Yorkshire, owned by Nelstrops.*

One of the things which the firm has done to ensure its survival is to work closely with the milling manufacturers. Co-operation with Satake UK, successor to Henry Simon, has led to the firm having the world's finest automated micro-chip controlled flour mills with continuous computerised on-line quality monitoring and full computer process control of wheat conditioning, cleaning and milling.

Nelstrops installed Satake's £3.2 million PeriTec system as a way to increase capacity within the existing mill buildings and provide the flexibility to increase its range of flours. The PeriTec milling system developed by Satake of Japan involves debranning wheat before milling. Debranning using both friction and abrasion can be varied according to the type of flour and bran required. The kernels are then passed through a hydrating unit designed to maximise water penetration and give a high level of control of moisture levels in the flour. Mainly used for milling hard wheat, the new technology has enabled Nelstrops to retain its edge over competitors.

Even slight variations in the flour can significantly affect dough making so it is vital to maintain strict performance parameters by detecting variations and compensating for them. Wheat from East Anglia for example is very different from Manitoban wheat grown in Canada and enzyme characteristics, starch damage and protein have to be adjusted to ensure consistent fermentation.

To maintain quality the firm has a laboratory containing the most sophisticated instruments available. Once a machine that tested flour for colour, protein content, starch damage, moisture and dough making characteristics needed eight hours for a full analysis; now with infra-red techniques the tests take only 30 seconds. The laboratory also remotely probes samples from each consignment of raw materials and remotely extracts samples from each bulk silo of the finished product. The final

Above: *The cover of a brochure issued by the firm in the late 1990s.*
Below: *One of the firm's fully automated state of the art computer systems.*

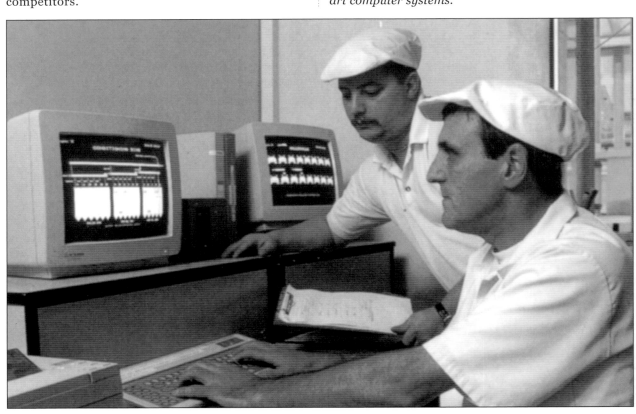

William Nelstrop's ran a small business with flexibility and a personal touch which is as evident today as it was then. Anyone wishing to speak to a director can do so: two members of the Nelstrop family are still part of the top management team in this the only independent family controlled flour mill in north west England, Scotland and Wales. All the directors have technical backgrounds and understand the importance of quality.

end-product whether loaf, pastry or mix is also rigorously assessed in the firm's Test Baking Plant.

During its existence Nelstrops has witnessed a revolution in 'logistics' from the canal and horse and cart to the steam driven lorry and the early internal combustion engine to the powerful tankers of today, which can swallow a 24 tonne load in mere minutes.

Today the mills' output is delivered by Nelstrops' own modern fleet of vehicles operated by King Brothers, a wholly owned subsidiary, known for its fast turnarounds and environmental awareness; the drivers, as the customers most frequent point of personal contact, pride themselves in being part of a family firm.

There are three mills on site including a facility for stone grinding, one of the mills is dedicated to wholemeal, and all are remodelled every five years or so. The firm's £2 million investment programme was designed to take the company well into the new millennium.

The Albion Mill still stands proud on Lancashire Hill but there is still room to expand on the site which has been steadily enlarged over the years as adjoining property became available. Ownership of the site has been an important factor in the firm's survival. Owning the premises outright and keeping them has meant that the firm has not had to spend money on moving to a green field site with the large capital investment which that would require.

The quest to achieve that quality starts with the firm's skill in sourcing the right kinds of wheat and ends not with the finished product but with excellent after sales service and technical back-up. It is no coincidence that the first line of Nelstrops' Mission Statement reads 'A commitment to quality is a key to survival' - a philosophy which has stood the firm in good stead down the decades.

Through an unbroken line of family control the business is now run by the fifth generation of Nelstrops: Conrad Nelstrop is chairman and was joint managing director with his cousin Paul Nelstrop until Paul's death early in 2000. Conrad Nelstrop's nephew Conrad Syers, the first of the sixth generation to be involved, is technical director whilst the chairman's son, Matthew works in the sales department. Milling has certainly changed a lot since 1820.

Above left: *The Quality Assurance Laboratory.*
Above right: *The mill roll floor in Mill No. 1.*
Right: *The directors in the 1990s (from left to right): Mr Conrad Nelstrop, Conrad Syers, Paul Nelstrop.*

Continuous production at Unity Mill

We've all heard of enzymes - but what on Earth are they? A firm that can readily supply the answer is Rhodia Ltd based at Unity Mill, Woodley. Enzymes are proteins which act as biological catalysts - making chemical changes happen faster and more efficiently than they would otherwise do. Enzymes exist in all life forms and are responsible for biochemical reactions in living organisms. Micro-organisms can be fermented to make a wide range of enzymes which can then be used to perform tasks in many everyday processes. The main advantage compared with other methods is that enzymes will only carry out the job they are designed for and nothing else. As a result they are easily controllable, and because they are proteins they are also totally biodegradable. Rhodia Food UK produce a range of food grade microbial enzymes at Woodley, for use in the food, brewing and animal feed industries, though many have a more general industrial application. The range includes enzymes used in starch processing (to produce glucose syrups), in animal feeds as improvers, in baking to enhance the rising of bread and the texture of dough and in the brewing industry to increase fermentability and improve clarification. Industrial applications include textile desizing (the removal of starch), leather production and effluent treatment.

Rhodia Ltd's 16 acre site at Woodley is situated in open countryside four miles east of Stockport. Originally a textile mill, today the building houses Rhodia's production plant, laboratories and offices as well as Rhodia's UK Northern Administration Centre. Production at the site is mainly concerned with the manufacture of microbial enzymes and malt extract.

Although the name Rhodia is relatively new, enzyme production on the site goes back for many decades under different names. The original business can be traced back to 1927 and to one Norman Evans who with his German partners, the Rais family, began importing enzymes to Britain from France.

Initially, the business involved supplying desizing enzymes to the textile industry but over the years other enzyme products have been developed for the starch, baking and brewing markets, and most recently for the animal feed industry. However, one new product, a cellulase enzyme, has turned full circle - back to the textile industry where it may be used in the manufacture of stone washed denim.

Below: *The 1952 annual dinner dance. Jack and Philip Evans are at the top table on the right hand side of the photograph.*

The Company originally traded from offices in Dudley Road, Whalley Range - the Evan's family home. The business was then concerned with supplying products to the local textile industry and amongst their product range were the desizing enzymes imported from France.

In the mid 1930s Norman Evans was joined in business by his two sons, Jack and Philip Evans. With their input the business expanded rapidly and they soon moved to new premises at Outwood House in Heald Green to provide space for the manufacture of their own products, particularly for the desizing enzymes. The Evans had watched the looming problems in Europe and correctly anticipated that sooner or later their French supplies would cease. Consequently, by the

start of the second world war the company had moved into manufacturing its own enzymes since they could no longer be imported. It was also during this period that the connection with the Rais family ended.

The manufacturing processes employed at Outwood House involved growing selected micro-organisms on the surface of a nutrient medium in shallow trays, a process known as surface culture fermentation. After the war the increase in demand for their products required the use of new fermentation technology, known as deep fermentation, where the microbes are grown in the nutrient medium in a stirred pressurised vessel - the fermenter. To develop this new process the firm had to move to larger premises to accommodate their new $4.5m^3$ fermenters.

Thus in 1952 Norman Evans and Rais Ltd moved production to Unity Mill - having bought the building in 1949 for £25,000. Unity Mill had been built in 1861 at the rear of Poleacre Lane. Originally named Trianon Mill it was constructed for use as a cotton spinning mill. However, by 1893 the four storey building was being used as a rubber works by the Hyde Imperial Rubber Company. In the early part of the 20th century it had reverted to cotton spinning and was owned by Mayall and Massey prior to its acquisition by Norman Evans and Rais Ltd.

Above: From left to right (back row) Phil Evans, Jack Evans. (Front row) Miss Stoddard (Company Secretary), Mrs Evans (wife of the founder, Norman Evans). Below: The premises in the 1970s.

In the 1960s the capital investment required to continue the expansion of the production facilities exceeded the Evans family's financial resources and therefore a friendly buyer was sought. After discussions with several potential buyers, Associated British Maltsters acquired Norman Evans & Rais Ltd and Unity Mill in 1964.

Now as a subsidiary of Associated British Maltsters Norman Evans and Rais Ltd was almost immediately combined with two other subsidiaries of ABM: British Diamalt Ltd and Sunvi Ltd, respectively manufacturers of malt extract and malt flour, and together with JM Colletts of Gloucester, they formed ABM Industrial Products Ltd with its headquarters at the Woodley site.

In 1972 ABM Chemicals, the group's new name, was incorporated into the Dalgety Food group - which was in turn acquired by RTZ Chemicals in 1986 and which was itself destined to became part of the Rhone-Poulenc Group three years later.

Today, as throughout the last 50 years, the deep fermentation process pioneered by NER continues to be employed at Woodley but the process now operates on the 15m^3 scale with significantly more sophisticated control of the process. During the fermentation the growth of the microbes is strictly controlled to maximise production of the desired enzyme which is then isolated, concentrated and formulated to give a liquid product with the designed performance. If a powdered product is required eg. for baking, then the liquid enzyme may be spray dried.

The principal raw materials used in the fermentation processes include sugars such as starch, glucose and cellulose and sources of protein such as yeast extract and corn steep liquor.

Enzymes are used in many industries, eg. in the conversion of starch to dextrins and sugars: in the food, brewing, and paper industries, for desizing in the textile industry, for protein modification in the food and brewing industries and in the leather industry for the preparation of skins for the tanner. They are also used in baking to modify the texture of dough. In addition to the enzymes, the company also manufactures a complete range of products for the brewing industry: something for each stage of the brewing process from vessel sterilants to beer foam stabilisers.

*Above: NER transport in 1961. **Top:** Norman Evans & Rais cricket team in 1950, members of the Stockport League.*

Alongside the usual Technical Service provided to all customers on the application of its products, the company offers an advisory service to the brewing industry, helping to address problems such as water treatment - by analysing the water used and defining the correct amounts of salts required to make specific types of beer. In addition, a range of malt extracts are produced at Woodley for use in the food and beverage industries which uses them in the production of meat pies, canned products, bread, beer, soft drinks, mince pies and Christmas puddings.

Following acquisition in 1989 by Rhone-Poulenc a year later Rhone-Poulenc's dairy business, Texel ,was transferred to Woodley followed by the Meyhall food thickener business in 1993.

In 1998 Rhone-Poulenc's chemical, fibres and polymers business combined to form a new speciality chemicals company called Rhodia. The Woodley site became part of that new company, now known as Rhodia Ltd.

Rhodia Food UK Ltd continues to manufacture and supply enzymes, malt extracts etc., from the Woodley site but the new company now has its main fermentation plant in France producing xanthan gums, organic acids and enzymes for the food and animal feed industries. So enzymes are again supplied from France as they were at the outset in 1927.

In addition to the production operation, Rhodia Food's Enzyme Research and Development Department is based at the site, working on the identification and developement of new enzymes for industry.

With around 150 employees working at Woodley, Unity Mill continues to make a significant contribution to the local economy 140 years after being built. Rhodia Food, the present owners, and its employees are totally committed to the chemical industry's Responsible Care Initiative, seeking continuous improvement in all aspects of the business from employee and public safety through to producing quality products and caring for the environment. Rhodia is an active member of the East Manchester Responsible Care Cell and all manufacturing operations are certified to internationally recognised quality standards.

Rhodia Food is especially concerned about the impact of its operations on the local community and therefore a Residents Liaison Committee, formed in 1992, meets regularly to ensure that any concerns of its neighbours are satisfactorily addressed.

With the potential use of enzymes ever on the increase we can be sure that Rhodia Ltd can look forward to a future ever bit as interesting as its past.

Above: *Enzyme processing - separation of biomass by centrifugation.*
Below: *Rhodia Ltd Unity Mill today.*

Phoenix from the flames

Not many businesses manage to grow from almost nothing to having sales amounting to hundreds of millions of pounds a year in just two decades. Of those which do, fewer still can have survived a disastrous fire or faced the destruction of much of their stock due to other unforseeable problems in their first year. One firm which has triumphed over such enormous difficulties to make itself one of the most important enterprises not only in Stockport but in the whole region is Parfetts, the family wholesaling firm.

AG Parfett & Sons Ltd, the cash & carry company, based in Didsbury Road began trading on 1st July 1980. The firm was founded by Alan Parfett and his wife Pat together with their eldest son Steve and originally operated from a 25,000 sq ft warehouse in Reddish. The couple's youngest son Robert joined the company in 1981. Daughters Barbara and Judy too have also worked for the firm with great success.

Before founding his own firm Alan Parfett had worked for various food companies since 1945 and had often thought of setting up in business for himself. The opportunity came in 1979 when a cash and carry unit in Reddish came on the market. Together with his family he decided to start the family business.

According to one staff member, who already worked at the warehouse when the Parfetts arrived, the existing staff were a little apprehensive because the place was very disorganised and there were hardly any customers. That apprehension was clearly misplaced: the family had big plans and things improved quickly; all of a sudden staff actually had customers and things to do! Arthur Ashton one of those first employees, and who would stay with the Parfetts for more than twenty years, recalls that being a family

Above: Alan and Pat Parfett, pictured here at the opening of the Stockport Depot extension.
Below: The original Parfetts Depot in 1980.

business meant everyone was required to help out in those early days. It was not unusual to see both Pat and Alan Parfett helping out with the cleaning up and making those ever important cups of tea alongside everyone else.

The first year was a hair raising time. Shortly after opening the doors Parfetts became victims of an Australian spider beetle infestation which meant the warehouse having to be closed down for an entire weekend with friends and family pitching in to help clear infected stock. The loss of sales and the destruction of stock cost over £5,000. At the end of that first year however the firm had still managed to make a profit of £500. Perhaps not a lot but enough to encourage the family which had not expected to see any profit for three years. Working seven days a week the family's hard work began to pay off. That did not mean they changed their economical ways however. When Pat Parfett noticed furniture missing from her house she didn't worry about burglars; she simply knew that Alan had been taking it to fill the ever expanding needs of the company office.

> *At the end of the first year the firm had managed to make a profit of £500*

The Reddish depot grew rapidly and by 1983 had become one of the busiest wholesale cash and carry outlets in the UK on the basis of sales per square foot.

In 1984 an extension of another 15,000 sq ft was added making the depot Manchester's premier cash and carry business. Things were looking good.

Disaster however struck in December 1986 when a fire destroyed the Reddish warehouse. The blaze which had been started by children playing in a skip took eleven fire engines to put out. The fire not only destroyed the building but also half of the Parfetts' stock.

Alan Parfett was woken at 4 am by his son Robert to be given the bad news. Robert and Steve had been there all night having themselves been told of the blaze by long-standing employee Lynda Livesey who had herself received a call from her brother saying the depot was on fire. Lynda had looked out of her bedroom window and seen the flames for herself. In the morning staff arrived to discover a terrible mess, they had to wear wellington boots and went home smelling of smoke, but they did what needed to be done. It could have been the end but the Parfetts made sure no one even lost a day's pay. Alan went to the office and assured the employees that their jobs were safe and that he would rebuild.

Disasters on such a scale would break many firms, indeed they would break many individuals. The Parfett family did not despair as so many others might have done. With true northern grit they pulled themselves together, assessed the damage and decided what needed to be done. And of course an awful lot did need to be done. Fortunately both family members and their dedicated employees were up to the task.

Above: *The fire at the Reddish Depot in 1986.*

A new warehouse of 60,000 sq ft was soon obtained adjacent to the motorway at Didsbury Road and within fourteen weeks Parfetts was back in business. Since then the Heaton Norris depot has had two extensions built bringing the total floor space to 100,000 sq ft.

In 1986 Parfetts bought a second warehouse unit, previously occupied by Courtaulds, and this time at Aintree. The new 82,000 sq ft depot was soon so successful that within five years it became inadequate and a new unit of 105,000 sq ft had to be built behind it at a cost of over £3 millions.

In 1988 the company won the first of many industry awards by being given the Independent Cash and Carry of the Year Award presented by the Independent Grocer magazine, an award which the company would go on to receive for four consecutive years.

In 1989 yet a third unit of 40,000 sq ft was acquired in Anfield and extensively modernised.

After almost a decade at the helm, in February 1989, Alan Parfett retired becoming chairman of the company whilst son Steve was appointed managing director assisted by his brother Robert, responsible for personnel, IT and marketing and financial director Robert Miller.

Alan's parting advice to his sons was that they would need to achieve £100 million in sales in the tenth year - and they did just that.

By 1991 the company was featured in the Independent on Sunday as one of the top fifty fastest growing private companies, one reason for that being made clear when the

Stockport depot was voted Britain's No. 1 Cash and Carry by off-licence retailers in a competition sponsored jointly by Courage and the Independent Grocer magazine. That same year, over in Anfield, the general manager there, Graham Jagger, won the Federation of Wholesale Distributors (FWD) Gold Medal Award as the Independent Cash and Carry Manager of the Year - a trend which would continue with awards being given in 1993 to Bill Pace who received an FWD gold medal for wholesale marketing achievements and Gary Kenwright winning a Checkout Award sponsored by Pro-Wholesaler magazine.

In 1994 Parfetts acquired the 117,000 sq ft Watson & Philip cash and carry business in Somercotes, Derbyshire. The following year Steve Parfett became chairman of Landmark, a voluntary wholesale group of which the firm had been an active member since being founded. Parfetts' fifth depot was acquired in 1998 through the purchase of a fellow Landmark member's business in Halifax, where less than two years later sales were up by 50 per cent.

Awards continued to be gained when in 1995 Andrew Kenny the firm's IT manager was awarded the FWD Gold medal for Information Technology Development. A year later the company was rated 49th out of 150 of the region's top companies in a Manchester Evening News survey. In 1997 John Chapman, the company marketing manager received the FWD President's Gold medal for outstanding services to the wholesale industry whilst in 1999 Peter Mullan general manager of Parfetts Stockport received the FWD Gold Medal for Manager of the year.

Below: *10th Anniversary celebrations in 1990, at Haydock Park.*

and competition from the supermarkets, Parfetts have succeeded in achieving growth in every one of their 20 years in business. They like to think that they have played a part in helping their customers to survive and prosper in the face of such competition. The five cash and carry depots operated today are amongst the most successful in the country, and the envy of many competitors.

During the first year of trading in 1980 the company had sales of £3 million and a staff of twelve; by 2000, the firms' twentieth year of trading, the company had grown to a business which employed 400 staff and enjoyed an annual turnover in excess of £200 million.

From the comfort of retirement Alan Parfett's greatest hope is that Parfetts will continue to grow steadily over the years and that, hopefully, one day his grandchildren will show an interest in joining the business ensuring that the firm continues to be a family concern.

In March 2000 Steve Parfett was elected chairman of the Federation of Wholesale Distributors, a position his father had held in the 1980s, the only example of both a father and son having held that prestigious post.

The company has changed almost beyond recognition in the 20 years since it was founded, and certainly surpassed the expectations Alan had when he decieded to 'go it alone'. However, its core busines continues to be the sale of goods strictly to trade customers, whether they be retail grocers, off-licences or newsagents, or catering customers running cafes, hotels or pubs. Despite the fact that this customer base, particularly the independent retailers, have faced enormous pressure

Above: *'Independent Grocer' Cash & Carry of the Year Award in 1988.* **Top:** *The opening of the Aintree Depot in 1986.* **Right:** *Robert Parfett, Steve Parfett and Robert Miller.*

Chances and changes

A Stockport company which is now confidently into its second century of trading in the printing industry began almost as a chance offshoot in the remarkable career of a remarkable man, Joseph Dean. Joseph was born in 1848, the son of a Yorkshire mill worker; his father was keen for his son to advance in business but his rather domineering attitude soon made the young Joseph determined to seek his fortune in any industry other than the woollen trade. He managed to escape his father's over-watchful eye but not his father's line of business as he answered an advertisement for a man required to take charge of a wool forming department of a hat works, the then famous Christy's hat factory in Stockport.

He worked for Christy's for a number of years but experience gained some years earlier, namely fluency in the French language, led to a turning point in his life when he organised a very successful trip to Paris for a group of Christy's employees. Shortly after this trip he was approached by the Manchester, Sheffield and Lincolnshire Railway with a view to him acting as their agent.

He was by this time a married man in his mid-twenties, with savings of a few hundred pounds behind him and he opened a small office in the Borough Chambers in High Street, Stockport in partnership with a Frenchman named Henry who had a tourist business in Oldham; the partnership was not a success however and Joseph Dean eventually bought him out. The railway company put Dean in touch with a fellow travel agent in Sheffield called Dawson and the company changed its name to Dean & Dawson (in Stockport) and Dawson & Dean (in Sheffield)!

Left: *Joseph Dean.*
Below and bottom: *Loading in the 1920s.*

GOVERNMENT CONTRACTORS

TELEPHONES 164 GATLEY MANCHESTER

TELEGRAMS "DEANSMERE." MANCHESTER

CODES:
A.B.C. 5TH EDITION.
BENTLEYS
MARCONI.

Dean & Co Spt Ltd

WHOLESALE MANUFACTURING STATIONERS,
Paper Merchants, Rotary & General Printers to the Trade.
COUNTER-CHECK BOOK MANUFACTURERS, DUPLICATE BOOK & LOOSE LEAF SPECIALISTS.

A source of considerable irritation and annoyance was that very often it proved difficult to have handbills, posters and other advertising matter printed in time, so Dean & Dawson acquired their own printing machine, so that their printing requirements could be satisfactorily met. It was this humble beginning which led to the company of Deanprint which we know today.

Joseph built up the business of Dean & Dawson with great judgment, determination and energy over many years. Its progress led it through being taken over by the railway company and its eventual dissolution once the railways were nationalised. This side of the business eventually became integrated into the Thos. Cook Travel Co.

Joseph Dean turned his considerable talents in another direction when after visiting America with a friend, local dignitary and hat-maker, Giles Atherton. While in New York they were offered the manufacturing rights of some hat leather stitching machines patented by a man named Bracher. The Bracher, Dean & Co Ltd was formed but was subsequently sued for an alleged breach of patent rights. During the course of litigation it was discovered that Bracher had not renewed his patents and therefore no infringement was possible.

This company became economically unviable when the price of stitching fell from 12s 6d a gross to about 2s

9d a gross. The company then started to make hat leathers and subsequently other leathers. In Stockport the printing and leather businesses were in three separate factories and it soon became obvious that the company should operate under one roof. The company sold the properties at Borough Chambers and the High Street and invested in the 47,000 sq ft factory in Cheadle Heath.

On 23 July 1920, two oak trees were planted on the site of the new works, one by Joseph Dean and the other by a man from the USA who was Mr Dean's first employee. This idea came from the fact that one of the original works had been called Royal Oak Works and it represented the continuity of the new from the old. These trees are standing and flourishing today.

During World War II, the works had a narrow escape. German bombs straddled the district and hit the building. But someone chalked up 'To hell with Hitler' and the works was in action again in two days.

Joseph Dean died in 1932, apart from his considerable business achievements, he had served the community as Councillor and Alderman, he was also Justice of the Peace for Stockport and for the County of Derbyshire. It is certain that this remarkable man would relish the very different challenges faced by Deanprint today, and take pleasure in the continuing success of the company he founded.

Above: *The Deanprint 1990 calendar.*
Top: *Letterhead engraving from the 1920s.*
Right: *The board of directors in 1990.*

A tradition of excellence

From simple beginnings, Chelwood Brick has become a leading player in the brick-making industry. The story began with the Harrisons and the Jacksons, who by the 1920s were established brickmakers in the Manchester Area. The company became known as J&A Jackson Ltd, incorporated on April 7th, 1922 with Joseph Jackson as Chairman. He was related to the Harrison Family by marriage. At its inauguration the company owned brickworks at Chorlton, Longsight, Bredbury, Reddish, Levenshulme, Denton and Adswood. In the first month of operation, the company was almost a millionaire, producing and selling nearly 1,000,000 bricks.

Over the next 50 years the company expanded and prospered by acquiring brickworks across North West England. Originally, the company's head office was in Longsight's Pink Bank Lane, moving to Swinton in 1974, before being stationed at the Adswood works in Cheadle.

A serious rift occurred in the mid 1930s, leading to Thomas Jackson being the last Jackson to be involved in the company. The Harrison family, who were important in the development of the company, were to see four generations of their dedicated and industrious clan making major contributions; from Thomas, the eldest of seven brothers involved, through to the flamboyantly dressed raconteur Walter, who retired from the company in 1996. In fact, it was James Harrison, the father of the seven brothers, who bought one of the first brickmaking machines, which caused riotous behaviour amongst hand brickworkers.

A new flag began to wave, when on December 5th 1973 Christian Salvesen took over the company. The name of J&A Jackson Ltd remained until June 1986, when it became Salvesen Brick Ltd.

Following a management buyout the name was changed to Chelwood Brick in May 1995. The name Chelwood reflected the company's location in Cheadle on Adswood Road. The name was chosen by way of a competition open to all company employees.

Above: *Brickmakers in the 1920s.*
Right: *A company van from the 1920s.*
Below: *The seven Harrison brothers.*

Manchester Airport meant that these were compulsorily purchased. However, the airport extension contractors were removing clay and depositing it on Jackson land for brickmaking and paying nine pence per cubic yard for the privilege. Small wonder one pays inflated prices for those trips to the Costas! On the subject of transport, like many companies founded in the 1920s, transport was primarily by horse and cart. This was followed by steamers, train and petrol wagons and by 1934, the transport fleet numbered nearly 200 vehicles. In 1976, the Longsight transport department closed, shortly after the entire transport fleet had been transferred to Transfleet and leasing was in operation.

The company recognised the value of its workforce and was not tardy in introducing benefits, such as service contracts and schemes for staff. In November 1933, Joseph Jackson paid a bonus of five pounds per week in which the output exceeded 300,000 bricks. This was achieved for 17 weeks and he met the cost of 85 pounds out of his own pocket.

The firm entered the second world war years with its records being placed in the basement of the Manchester Calico Printers Association building. Throughout the duration much land was sequestered for air raid shelters. A large part of the transport fleet and many excavators were on hire to different ministries up and down the country. On a truly sad personal note, the Chairman's eldest son, Peter Harrison was killed over the capital in a Spitfire. However, throughout the hostilities, the company never closed. It was important to look to the future, for by 1943 plastic building materials and prefabricated houses were being openly discussed. Needless to say these provoked much discussion at board meetings. A Jackson's property at Heaton Mersey Farm attracted some of Hitler's bombs, rendering some buildings a total loss under the War Damage Act and in November 1947 a settlement of 800 pounds resulted.

An important factor in successful brickmaking is the acquisition of suitable claybearing land. Purchase of land causes numerous problems, such as protracted negotiations with the landowners. In March 1937, 10 acres and one rood were bought for £2,000 from the Vicar of Atherton.

The company accumulated good clay bearing land around Ringway village and the hungry demands of

Throughout its history, Chelwood Brick has responded to commercial pressures by keeping abreast of developments and investment in plant and processes, such as in kiln technology and energy efficiency.

The brickmaking industry has long been subject to a rise and fall in demand and the company has always responded with a range of effective measures. From 1991 to 1992, national demand fell by 12 per cent, yet the firm's sales fell by only 2.8 per cent, with its market share rising from 3.6 per cent to 5.5 per cent.

The company boasts, 'A brick for all reasons.' With a wide range of wire cuts, genuine hand-mades and traditional stocks included in its product portfolio, one can understand their boast.

Chelwood Brick leads the way in the use of state of the art manufacturing and fully computerised process control technology. This enables the company to offer exceptional product quality. Chelwood offers comprehensive sales and technical support, computer aided design and special shaped brick facilities, the company claims the best customer service in the industry.

Above left: *Brickmaking today.*
Above right: *High output brick setters.*

The Stockport company with designs on the world

A history of excellence and innovation in the reinforced concrete construction industry commenced in 1918 when Simon Carves Reinforced Concrete department started in Mount Street in Manchester and moved to Birdhall Lane, Stockport in 1934. Throughout the following years the company has been at the forefront of design of concrete structures in many areas of application from the coal industry to offshore installations and in places as far apart as Libya and the USA.

Former distinguished members of staff include Charles Reynolds who was compiler of the professional bible The Reinforced Concrete Designers Handbook (first published 1932).

Above centre: *Birdhall Lane in the mid 1920s.*
Below: *A service bunker for a coke oven instal-lation in 1937.*

During the 1940s the company was involved in coal washeries and coke oven construction and employed a number of Polish engineers and draughtsmen who had been demobilised in the UK after the end of World War II. It pioneered continuously moving form-work using a slipforming technique at Portishead using hand-jacks in the 1950s. During this time Simonbuild and Simonconsult were formed and the Simon-Carves expertise was sought for design solutions in concrete structures for buildings, bunkers, silos, water towers, reservoirs, bridges, retaining walls, chimneys and foundations.

The 1960s saw the company involved in the use of revolutionary building materials; it made fibreglass shutters and used epoxy resins in construction work; it was also was involved in the development of an epoxy injected prestressing anchorage. Under the name GEC-Simon-Carves consortium they were the first to handle nuclear power station design in 1961 on the Hunterston

A project; they were also the first in the UK to construct a prestressed concrete reactor pressure vessel. The BBRV technique was used in the construction of, among other things, M5 bridges and also for making tendons used in the repair to Norwich Cathedral.

Exploration in the North Sea oil and gas fields in the 1970s led to the application of the prestressing and slip forming procedures to the Cormorant offshore platform. At this time also the company was involved in building cable structures - these included the Lyne bridge and grandstands for Abu Dhabi, Twickenham and Goodwood.

The year 1980 saw the opening of a new chapter in the history of the company when it became part of Multi (UK) which led to a new emphasis on a multi-disciplinary approach to design which is a hallmark of its present operations.

A management buy-out by the Directors and staff in April 1991 established the present-day company Multi Design Consultants Ltd (MDC) as a practice of consulting engineers, architects and project managers. The company is able to provide a complete design service for all building projects and has an extensive client base in the north west, whilst nationally it is able to provide a specialist service to the pharmaceutical, nuclear and defence industries. In 1994 the company moved to its present offices in Regal House, in the centre of Stockport, thus drawing to a conclusion the long association with the early Simon origins on Birdhall Lane.

The multi-discipline approach is demonstrated by a sample of projects undertaken since that date, which include a new oxide fuel complex at Springfields for British Nuclear Fuels and a coke oven by-product plant in Detroit, USA. More recent projects in this region are as diverse as a new clad-rack pallet silo for Gallaher in Crewe, which is one of the largest in Europe, and a ferro-cement sculpture for Salford City Council, forming one of the exhibits along the Irwell Valley Sculpture Trail.

Perhaps no project demonstrates the capabilities of the company better than the construction of a new distribution centre at Sherwood Park for Boots the Chemists. The centre, completed six weeks ahead of schedule in April 1998 was named best commercial building and overall winner by a panel of national judges in a competition run by the Manchester Society of Architects - the practice's winning design was competing against Marks & Spencer's landmark Manchester store and the Vasco da Gama shopping centre in Lisbon, both award winning schemes in their own right.

Top left: *A typical 1940s project.* ***Above left:*** *The oxide fuels complex for BNFL, Springfields.*
Above right: *The Grandstand at Goodwood, opened in 1980.* ***Below:*** *Today's directors.*

Nearly a century of family education

Ramillies Hall School has been run by the same family for over 80 years, preparing pupils for entry to local independent schools and boarding schools nation-wide, as well as for local state schools. The origins of the school can be traced to 1884 when a Mr Cox founded a school at Haw Bank, Cheadle. In 1919, after the death of Mr Cox, Mr RN Patterson, who had previously taught at Melton Mowbray, took over the school. Only a few days later he received a letter from a Dr Godson in Cheadle offering the use of Cheadle House, which had been used as a military hospital during the first world war. Mr Patterson agreed and later that year the school was opened. It was intended to be a school to prepare boys for 'our great public schools'. Although Cheadle House did have reasonably large grounds, sporting activity was carried out at a number of sites around the village. The relative lack of traffic passing through the village meant that it was quite easy, and safe, for a group of boys to be taken to sports fields.

In the spring term of 1920 the school had to close three weeks early due to an epidemic of whooping cough. Great change was to come at the beginning of the 1921/22 term when the girls' school was created, albeit as a separate school initially. In 1933 the school's physical activities were augmented by the formation of a scout troop, based in the old stabling and wash-house block at the rear of the cottage. Camping equipment was bought and regular expeditions were launched to many areas of Britain, a

Above centre: *Part of the original building at the north side of the school.*
Below left: *Early cookery classes.*
Below right: *Over the years the school has won many trophies for its sporting achievements.*

In 1946 Mr Patterson's son, Kenneth (CKM) Patterson, succeeded him on his return from war service with the Royal Marines. He was joined as head of the school by Mr Desmond Clements. The two had met at the Royal Marine office at the Admiralty. During the Patterson/Clement years the school expanded further with new buildings provided and old ones improved; a swimming pool was also built with the help of parental contributions. Both retired in 1979 after 33 years working together. Mr Patterson moved to Shetland and Mr Clements to Penzance.

In recent years the school has continued to expand with the opening of the nursery in 1981. The school now caters for boys and girls between the ages of six months and 13 years and is the only preparatory school in Greater Manchester to offer boarding. There are currently around 200 pupils with about 20 boarders. The school also specialises in the teaching of dyslexic children and is recommended by the Dyslexia Institute, further augmenting the school's local and international reputation.

The Patterson family is still involved in the running of the school. On the retirement of CKM Patterson, his daughter Anne took over the administration of Ramillies and in 1984 her sister Diana joined her as Principal in charge of the educational aspects of the school.

particular favourite being the Outer Hebrides. By 1934 the traffic in Cheadle village had increased to the point where it became more and more difficult to lead the boys safely to their playing fields. The decision was taken to relocate the school and after some searching this led to the discovery of Ramillies Hall, which had been a family home and farm owned by the Rostron's. It had been empty for a number of years and is reported, by Mr CKM Patterson, to have resembled a haunted house. The main building was converted into accommodation for the boarders, whilst the class-rooms have been purpose built amongst flower beds and trees on the south side of the grounds. The school stands in nine acres of grounds with fields on three sides, one of which has been drained and converted into playing fields.

Most of the masters joined the forces during the war, as did many of the old boys. This left teaching duties at the school in the hands of elderly men and the physically unfit.

Above: *Cricket on the playing field at Ramillies.*
Top left: *From stable yard to courtyard - now one of the children's play areas.*
Top right: *Computer classes - 1980s style.*
Right: *The school from the air.*

Laying down the law

Sooner or later we all require the services of a solicitor; perhaps to help make a will, to buy property or deal with a difficult divorce - or even, Heaven forbid, because we have fallen foul of the law.

The need for legal specialists has existed since classical times and lawyers are friends indeed when help is needed to get the layman through the maze of the British legal system. In England lawyers have historically been divided into two camps, barristers and solicitors, the former are courtroom specialists who would not see a client without referral from a solicitor, the latter acting as 'general practitioners' dealing with a wide range of clients and referring to barristers in the more difficult cases. Today that job demarcation is gradually being eroded with solicitors frequently specialising themselves, appearing in court and forming ever larger partnerships. One of Stockport's most prominent firms of solicitors is that of Sinclair Abson Smith.

The firm's story began in the 1930s when two young solicitors James Abson and David Taylor had the courage to set up in partnership in Princes Street, Stockport. Concentrating mainly on property and trust work they built up a good reputation and in 1958 they again showed their courage by moving to Greek Street where John Berry joined them. The popular view then was that they were moving out into the wilderness, but they were soon vindicated when Greek Street later became an enclave of solicitors, accountants, estate agents and valuers.

In 1954 solicitor Malcolm Hall had set up on his own in the Market Place and later took into partnership his pupil, Neville Holt. Together they earned a reputation for family work, crime, licensing and general litigation. Malcolm Hall was also Clerk to the Cheshire County Justices for the Petty Sessional Division of Stockport.

It was apparent that the services provided by both firms complemented each other and in 1968 Abson Taylor Berry & Co and Malcolm Hall became Abson Hall based in Greek Street. The new firm blossomed and when the property boom was at its height Abson Hall had three offices in Stockport, one in Wilmslow and one in Macclesfield with 13 solicitors and over 100 support staff. In 1990 the firm was further strengthened by the acquisition of the old established firm of Barlow Parkin & Co.

Above: *The partners in Abson Hall at the retirement party for Mr Hall, held in the wardroom of the Falklands War veteran HMS Plymouth.*

As clients' needs changed; as legislation became progressively more voluminous and complex; with the advance of technology and as specialisation became more and more essential the firm was reorganised by centralising offices and creating specialist departments.

By 1990 there were seven firms of solicitors in Greek Street, one of which, occupying two offices, had been started in Great Underbank by Ernest Higginbottom just after the second world war. He had been joined by Mr White, establishing the firm of Higginbottom & White which had also migrated to Greek Street. The Higginbottom family developed the practice until 1994 when the then remaining partners Philip Smith and Sandra Sinclair re-established under the name Sinclair Smith. By 1999 Sinclair Smith had grown to six solicitors and was expanding rapidly. The two firms Abson Hall and Sinclair Smith were almost duplicates in the services they offered clients and so it came as no surprise when they merged to form today's firm of Sinclair Abson Smith. With 19 solicitors and 30 support staff the present firm epitomises the change in delivery of professional legal services over the last seventy years. The journey from central Stockport to Greek Street, from the ink pen to e-mail, from brass plates to web sites is complete and appropriate to the opening years of a new century.

> *The end result of the merger is a well balanced firm, offering every kind of legal advice needed*

The end result is a well balanced firm covering all departments, able to offer the services of specialists in commercial and company work, family law, employment law, licensing, personal injury, domestic and commercial conveyancing, probate and trust work and general litigation. The quality of the solicitors is illustrated by the fact that from their ranks have come one Assistant Recorder, four District and Deputy Judges, one Magistrates' Clerk and four Tribunal Chairmen.

The day of the one-man family lawyer is now largely a memory. But Sinclair Abson Smith can still proudly recall its past, even as it looks to the future.

Top: *The staff of Abson Hall waiting outside the offices for the Queen to drive along Greek Street on 21st June 1977.*

Bringing new life to old mills

The Peak group of companies began life when the Gwinnett family left Cardiff for the North west in 1962. Ken, the father of the family, had the idea of selling gas appliances on commission for The North West Gas Board. The company began trading from a small showroom in Hazel Grove, funded by the £300 Ken had brought with him from South Wales.

The company, then known as Peak Gas Limited, grew rapidly. When the new American split level cookers were introduced, the unions at the Gas Board refused to install them as a joiner would be needed to complete the work. To get around this problem the Chairman of the North West Gas Board offered the contract for the whole of the North West to Peak Gas. The company seized this opportunity with relish and further expanded into fitted kitchens. This led to them supplying the Gas Board, Norweb, Manweb and the Midlands Electricity Board. For the next 25 years Peak Gas became the Authorised Agents for the board, further expanding their business to include fitted bathrooms and central heating. As the business expanded so did their staff, until they were employing around 150 workers.

By the early 1980s the family's business had expanded so much that they had outgrown their premises. The search for new premises led to an on-spec visit to

Right: *Brook Street Works at Hazel Grove.*
Below: *Albion Mill, the 19th century mill.*

Arrowscroft mill in Glossop which was about to shut down. A deal was quickly struck and the mill purchased for £55,000. This gave the family a site of around 80,000 square feet., much more than the 6,000 square feet they needed, for around half the price of building their own site. The family partitioned off the area they needed leaving them with around 74,000 square feet of space on a six acre site. Soon afterwards they began to be approached by small companies asking if they could rent the remaining space. The family quickly realised that there was a demand for relatively small industrial spaces and within two years they had managed to completely let the remaining floor space.

Having realised that they had stumbled upon a good business opportunity the family bought more mills in Hyde and Hollingworth.

The company's next major project came with the Goyt Mill in Marple. The mill which opened in 1907 had gone through a number of owners since its closure in 1960 and was again empty in the early 1980s. The then owners of Goyt Mill, Kay Metzlers, wanted to knock the mill down and use the land for housing. Backing the Peak Groups' determination to save the mill building were local residents, newspapers and the planning department as the council wanted jobs not houses.

Today Goyt Mill is the flagship of the Peak Group of Companies, housing their headquarters along with such diverse businesses as a climbing wall, a gym and an A La Carte restaurant. As well as housing a variety of businesses the mill is also the home of Hector the Ghost, although as yet he has failed to appear on any of the companies security cameras. The mill was also the starting place for a well-known local radio station in its early days as a pirate station.

Top: *Goyt Mill, originally a cotton mill.*
Above: *Pennine View Estate.*
Right: *London Road.*

This saw the premises being regularly raided by the Home office. Eventually a concrete bunker with secret entrances was built in the basement to allow the station workers to flee before capture!

The Goyt Mill site has been further expanded by the building of 12 new industrial units next to the mill in brickwork designed to blend their surroundings in order to preserve the heritage of the mill. Sadly, though, the mill has not escaped entirely intact since the Peak Group took over the site. The Mill's chimney had to be demolished in 1985 as it was becoming unstable. The chimney had been a local landmark since its construction in 1905. Its most famous feature being its two white bands, known locally as Gertie's Garters.

The Peak Group of companies are still family owned and are now run by Ken's three son's Paul, Mark and Karl Gwinnett and their two sons, who have become company directors. The family business continues to expand with a group of limited companies including the original Peak Gas Limited, as well as offshore interests. The company is now estimated to be worth somewhere in the region of 18-20 million pounds.

Recycle - it's vital

Not too long ago we threw everything away. Now, more environmentally conscious, we recycle. But recycling in Stockport has a surprisingly long history. 'Recycle It Is Vital' is the motto of Stockport's long-established family firm, Elsa Waste Paper Ltd. The company's Mission Statement being 'to promote a greener Stockport by preventing as much landfill possible'. No-one can argue with that.

Today, amongst other activities, the company collects waste paper, compresses and bales it and returns it to paper mills for recycling.

The business was founded in 1954 by husband and wife, Douglas and Elsie Morgan. Douglas, one of 15 children and Elsie one of 14, must have learned quite a bit about re-cycling in their childhood.

Whilst working as bus driver Douglas Morgan had begun a small sideline from his home at 4 Astley street Stockport collecting waste cardboard after seeing so much of it around the streets of Stockport.

After amassing a pile of unwanted cardboard Douglas contacted Thames Board, a firm in Warrington, which agreed to buy anything he collected. Douglas sold the family's three piece suite in order to buy a van and started collecting even more waste. It was just as well that the suite had been sold - they needed the space since the cardboard was stored in the front room until there was enough to take to Warrington.

Douglas Morgan eventually left the buses and started full time in the waste cardboard business with his wife Elsie joining him doing a little of everything. Douglas began collecting cardboard just from local businesses but he was soon making collections throughout the

Above: Doug and Elsie Morgan on their wedding day. ***Below:*** *Doug Morgan in India during World War II (second from right).*

The fact that the company has been in existence for so long means that it has many loyal customers - still including the Co-op, the firm's first large client.

Times have changed since Douglas Morgan bought his first small van. Today the firm has ten vehicles and 16 staff and uses roll-on roll-off lorries to make collections throughout the region. In addition to collecting waste paper the firm also provides a confidential document shredding service - and if necessary removes waste for landfill.

With a new baling machine of the most modern American manufacture - one of the largest in the business and a second one is being thought of - the firm is now set to continue its mission into its second half century. Elsa Waste Paper is also now diversifying, collecting plastic waste before baling it and sending it to China for re-use.

north west; his first large contract however was from the Co-op.

The Morgans soon rented a garage at The Pineapple Inn and ran their business from there for a few months until they eventually moved to Gas Street, under the railway arches, where the firm would stay until 1968.

When in 1968 the firm left the railway arches it moved to premises in Station Road, Reddish, a location where it would stay for more than 30 years until Easter 2000 when the business moved across the road to its present, much larger premises, at Units 1-4, Station Road on the Station Industrial Estate.

In the year following the move to Reddish, the Morgans were joined by Ron Humphreys. Ron was the fiancé of Douglas and Elsie's daughter Cynthia; he became a partner bringing new ideas with him which would help take the business forward to new heights.

Although the business has grown and matured over the decades of its existence, that growth has not been without its hiccups. The firm has survived a number of crises in its history, not least seven fires. Fire is a major hazard wherever paper is stored: each of the company's fires was the result of local children playing with matches.

Douglas Morgan died in 1982 and his daughter Cynthia joined the business. Today Cynthia Humphreys runs the firm together with her two sons Greg and Nick whilst Ron Humphreys is now managing director of Cheshire Recycling in Ellesmere Port.

Greg Humphreys' twin boys will hopefully one day carry on the business. Cynthia is looking forward to handing the business over to Greg and Nick when she retires, followed eventually by the fourth generation of the family which has done so much to maintain our environment.

Above: *Doug with his comrades in India (top centre).*
Right: *Cynthia and Ron Humphreys' wedding.*

'V for Victory'! Residents of School Street celebrate the end of the war in Europe on 30 May 1945.

SCHOOL ST
V·E·DAY----
CHILDREN'S
CELEBRATION.

Acknowledgments

The publishers would like to thank Stockport Libraries for the use of their pictures in this book

Thanks are also due to
Raymond Clayton who penned the editorial text
and Judith Dennis and Steve Ainsworth for their copyywriting skills